RETIREMENT'S
MISSING LINK

RETIREMENT'S
MISSING LINK

WHAT WALL STREET *DOESN'T* TELL YOU AND MAIN STREET *OVERLOOKS*!

John Lewandoski, CRC

Golden Years Publishing
Pennsylvania, USA
www.personal-retirement-planning.com

Retirement's Missing Link—What Wall Street Doesn't Tell You and Main Street Overlooks, **1st Edition.** Copyright © 2012 by John Lewandoski. Manufactured in the United States of America. All rights reserved. No part of this book may be reproduced or transmitted in any form or by any means, electronic or mechanical, including photocopying, recording, or by any information storage or retrieval system—except by a reviewer, who may quote brief passages in a review to be printed in a magazine, newspaper, or on the Web—without permission in writing from the publisher. For information, please contact Golden Years Publishing, 2062 County Line Road, East Greenville, PA 18041, or contact us by email on our website: www. personal-retirement-planning.com

Although the author and publisher have made every effort to ensure the accuracy and completeness of information contained in the book, we assume no responsibility for errors, inaccuracies, omissions, or any inconsistency herein. Any slights of people, places, or organizations are unintentional. All book content is for informational purposes only; the author and publisher assume no responsibility for any action resulting from any stated information contained herein.

Edited by Dr. James Arcieri and David Lewandoski
Cover Design and Interior Layout by Daniel MacBride

Published by Golden Years Publishing, 2062 County Line Road, East Greenville, PA 18041

ISBN: 978-0-9832243-0-3

Library of Congress Control Number: 2011929837

Library of Congress Cataloging- in-Publication Data:
Lewandoski, John
Retirement's Missing Link—What Wall Street Doesn't Tell You and
    Main Street Overlooks
Paperback, 8½ x 5½ x ¾ , 280 pages, extensive Table of Contents,
    glossary

ATTENTION—CORPORATIONS, PROFESSIONAL ORGANIZATIONS, COLLEGES, LIBRARIES, and others: Quantity discounts are available on bulk purchases of this book for educational or gift purposes, or as premiums for increasing magazine subscriptions or renewals. *Special books or book excerpts can also be created to fit specific needs.* For more information, please utilize the email located on our website:

www.personal-retirement-planning.com

Dedication

This book is dedicated to the principle of retirement support, and to the family of people with whom I share common ground in generational life development: The Baby Boomer Generation.

It is especially dedicated to those who take later-life seriously enough to pursue their own life course and, in so doing, bypass narrow retirement mediocrity so prevalent within our culture. I applaud your foresight and enthusiasm!

Acknowledgments

The initiative to write *Retirement's Missing Link* was born in conversation with a friend, Brian Middleton—entrepreneur, successful business owner, and all-around knowledgeable, insightful individual. Several years ago, a time when I was especially considering starting some sort of ministry or business centered on retirement and later life in general, Brian came into my sphere of close acquaintances.

His willingness to help, and encouragement to share my own insights on the mature phase of life, provided impetus I needed. This book and my retirement consulting business are primarily attributable to Brian's encouragement.

Ask my wife. Audrey understands living with a writer whose mind, for several years, has heavily focused on communicating with the hearts of others—the Boomer Generation. I sincerely thank Audrey for graciously allowing my hold-up in 'the study' all this time (and thank you, Doll, for your forgiveness when I've overdone it).

Dan MacBride's artistic and graphic capabilities have been crucial in piecing together, in cyberspace and ultimately in print, the thoughts in my head. In the beginning he said to me, "You write the book; I'll worry about putting it together.

Dr. Jim Arcieri's actual editing and editorial suggestions have shown sensitivity, depth of knowledge, and experience, all of which have contributed to general book direction.

Dave Lewandoski, my son, has factored integrally in editing, as his sharp insight and younger generational viewpoint has provided angle of perspective I couldn't have possibly seen on my own. (The child can be father to the man at times.)

I'm most grateful to my God for seemingly countless influences over the years which have culminated in any of the good that may result from this book and my consulting business in general. The assemblage of input from people in the fields of education, the corporate world, and Christian ministry, to say nothing of life eventualities in general—I believe all to have been guided by a Hand far more creative and powerful than my own....

Lastly, thank you, my reader, for your purchase of this book, and for possessing the faith I've something of merit to offer you in your admirable quest toward later-life preparation. May it so be.

About the Author

I dislike writing about myself. But I *more* dislike writing about myself in the traditional manner of third person; i.e., "*John* is a personal retirement consultant who…," etc. Others have suggested having another write about me, the author.

It seems if another describes the author, the heart of the author isn't really being presented. The whole approach seems cock-eyed, a little disingenuous. If the author describes self, it can appear self-crowing. Please allow me, therefore, to tell you about 'me' to the degree it reflects on this book and your relationship to me through it.

Real Credentials:

The simplest yet comprehensive bio I can provide merges a mix, from antiquity, of multiple and diverse university studies coupled with nearly fifty years of life experience largely within the corporate structure of business management, the church, and family life. Does all this 'qualify' me to expound on sensitive life issues, such as how to live later-life, and to provide advice that can genuinely help others along those lines? You'll have to be the judge. Tell me—which doctor or attorney is more qualified—the new graduate, or that same person with fifty years accumulated life experience?

I know a lot about little, but a little about a lot. That's my qualifier. Let me speak to the heart of the boomer, not from an academic litany of Ph.D. credentials, but from a heart of experience, keen observation, and considerable systematic thought and study, whose results have been proven to work in the lives of others.

For years I've sensed there is merit in combining genuine life experience with self-originating areas of expanded interest: gerontology, philosophy, psychology, religion, science and sociology. It's that blend of interest and decades of corporate/public life that together qualify me to talk about both the generation of which I'm part—The Boomer Generation—and those who live within it, my boomer contemporaries.

Maybe Credentials:

Certification as a professional retirement consultant; owner of my own publishing business; decades of heavy participation in corporate management; raising a family; being a believer that truth is more important than political correctness; possessing die-hard passion to write, to communicate; having had works published in *Country* and *Pennsylvania Magazine*; possessing many unpublished works people tell me I should 'have published'. Maybe most of all, considerable encouragement to write and publish *Retirement's Missing Link*—the book you are holding:

> "Write the book, John, and get it published! We know you have something to say and there's an entire boomer culture needing to hear it!"

So…, on that encouraging admonition from only a handful of people I highly respect, so I publish. May it be an enjoyable, edifying read for you.

Foreword

We've all seen them. Financial firms are spending millions these days on commercials targeting the "Baby Boomer generation" as they prepare for retirement. Whether it's a commercial or a slogan about 'knowing your (retirement) number', 'retiring on your terms' or 'staying on a green line', they all have one thing in common; a focus on your dollars and how to not only preserve them but help them grow so they might last so you can live financially comfortable in retirement.

Being a Certified Financial Planner (CFP®), I can honestly tell you management of the boomer's life savings has been, and will remain the key focus of the financial planning community. Planners and their clients often talk through their picture of retirement, discuss their goals, objectives, and risk tolerance. Using any of the various financial planning computer software available, the planner runs through probability calculations to determine the likelihood the client will meet their goals and if their money might last as long as they live. Planners build a financial plan with the client, and then through regular reviews work to help clients stay on the right path. Your financial house, however, is really just half your retirement story.

At any bookstore or Amazon, you'll find hundreds of books on finances, investing, financial planning, and retirement planning with a focus on leisure. Try to find a book that can help the individual establish genuine self examination to get them truly thinking about whether they are truly emotionally ready—*that kind of information is hard to find.*

That's why I endorse, and plan to present to my clients, the book you are about to read because it provides counsel on the equally important emotional side of the retirement story.

Real Balance for Boomers

When John Lewandoski invited me to provide a foreword to *Retirement's Missing Link,* at first I wondered if what he was offering the boomer culture had real value. You'll find this isn't a direct 'how-to' book. It's one that leads you into *your own* retirement preparation. Planners help boomers with their financial *plan;* John helps them personally *prepare.*

John's guidance identifies two important and often overlooked keys to successful retirement. The first is understanding that moving from career to retirement is bigger and more personally complex than anticipated. The second is getting boomers to actually become aware of the need for personal later-life preparation.

Something's Missing

The various definitions I've heard over the years for "retirement" can almost unanimously be summed up as *"the ability to do whatever it is you want to do, whenever you want to do it."* This leisure focused definition encapsulates these two main ideals for retirees; financial independence, and freedom from punching the 9–5 clock.

Where I believe the financial community could do so much more is filling in the 'second half' of the retirement plan. Is the client psychologically and emotionally ready to walk away from a career that has defined them for 20–30 years, and step into the great unknown of retirement and the freedom it could provide?

I have found many of those initially excited about retirement soon realize playing golf three or four times a week can get stale, sitting at the pool or beach and reading books can get boring, and traveling really eats into that nest egg. Moreover, their new retirement zip code may seem a little lonely without their friends, to say nothing of distance from their family and grandkids. These folks thought, and believed, they were ready to retire once their investment plan rolled out the 'green line'. They often fail to really look deeply into their soul to properly define what retirement would mean outside the financial and leisure aspects.

The Right Tool for the Job

From my perspective, John's work impressively centers on the issues pre-retirees face from their psychologically personal side—struggles a financial planner is not professionally qualified to handle.

John presents a novel and particularly valuable retirement tool—the Retirement Success Profile (RSP). The RSP will dramatically help sift through all the personal and practical reasons involved in migrating from decades of career/mid-life into post-career experience. So, perhaps even more importantly, the RSP and John's personal guidance will help you make a more rational, personal analysis of how well you will prepare for what could be another 20–30 or hopefully more years of active life.

For all that financial institutions put into their marketing to highlight their services; I believe there is another critical personal half to the retirement story. John's book, his RSP, and consulting skills help to fill the void. They connect the financial and emotional pieces of retirement planning—completing the retirement picture for you. The tools are here, but it is up to *you!*

Studies have shown that most pre-retirees spend more time planning a vacation than planning for their own retirement:

- Don't be a statistic!
- Do your own research!
- Find a Certified Financial Planner and build a plan!
- Finish reading this book and work through the RSP with John, and be better prepared for all life and retirement may entail.

Buckle up—it could be a complex, bumpy ride. But, also one you can, and need to enjoy! Now, let's get to work!

J. Ryan Forbrich works with Financial Planning Services, a team oriented full service financial planning firm based in Northern Virginia. By teaming with John and his RSP process, Ryan hopes to help pre-retirees complete their retirement picture so they can successfully enjoy their Golden Years.

Ryan holds the designation CERTIFIED FINANCIAL PLANNER™ Professional, as well as being an Investment Advisor Representative with ING Financial Partners. ING Financial Partners is not associated nor affiliated with John Lewandoski.

For further information and help in completing your retirement picture, Ryan can be reached at Ryan@MakingMoneySense.com or 703-330-3100.

Table of Contents

Foreword x

General Book Focus.. 1

Common Ground.. 2

PART I: Addressing Retirement Realities

Chapter 1: Don't Get Old 7
Ma's Advice on Aging • Becoming Old; Not Being Old • The Elderly at Pennswood Village • Getting Serious About It All • Peer Indifference Further Piqued Interest

Chapter 2: Why You Need This Book 13
To Acquire Missing Personal Retirement Needs which are • To Learn Balanced Realty for Later Life • To Go the Distance • Welcome • Written Mainly for Two Groups of People • War & Winning • Gaining Initial Retirement Bearings • Pre-retirement Angst • Retirement Success Profile—Your Best Wake-up Call

Chapter 3: Critical Questions... 21
Upfront Reality Questions • Getting Started

Chapter 4: Reliable Statistics and What They Mean 27
Ameriprise Financial Tells It Like It Is • New Retirement Mindscape, 2005/2006 • New Retirement Mindscape II, 2010 • NIH Senior Health—on Senior Depression • Turning Negative to Positive Advantage • No Silver Bullet—'Disclaimer' • Financial Planners— Essential (but not the whole story) • Two Different Doctors • Get Certified • It's Not Just Ameriprise Financial

Chapter 5: Lop-sided Reality... 44
Current Retirement Thinking • Later-life Aversions • Why We Avoid the Unlovely • What to Do • Why All This Negative Focus

Chapter 6: Feelings—and the Need for Truth 54

Feelings, Emotions and Truth • Truth Gets Things in Order • We Can Be Our Own Problem

Chapter 7: Social Pathology and Big Business— Bad Combination 60

Boomers—a Spoiled Generation? • Sick Boomers? • Social Pathology and Big Business- Bad Combination • The Retirement 'Industry' • The Retirement Sales Message

Chapter 8: Time, Aging, and Retirement: Inextricably Connected 71

Brief Thoughts on Time and Aging • Critical Focus in Retirement • No Time for Aging • Time Delivers Both Life and Death

Chapter 9: The Paradox of Retirement and Aging 76

The Big Umbrella • Retirement: Paradise or Paradox—Making Sense of It All • Societal Culture Fuels the Paradox • How Shall We Then Live?

Chapter 10: The Complexity of Time and Aging 84

Avoiding Back Trouble • Discipline Thine Self! • Belief: How We Each Perceive Aging • Is Aging Necessarily Bad or Negative? • Why We Age • Another View of the Aging Phenomenon

Chapter 11: Aging's Positives 100

Graceful Aging • Retirement: A Gateway to Clear Thought • Letting Time Sliiiiide… • More Good Things • The Cynic

Chapter 12: Crossroads, Decisions, Building Roadblocks 108

Life Crossroads • The Battlefield is the Mind • The Ghost of Retirement— Yet to Come • Life Crossroads Requiring Decision and Courage • Mind Focus Counters Aging's Deceptions • Aging Deception: I Can't Do Things Anymore • Aging Deception: I See Myself as Old—All I've Done is Now Lost • Building Our Own Defensive Roadblocks

Chapter 13: Good Decisions 123

Dealing With Decisions • Intuitive or Analytical Decision Making: Which is Best?

Chapter 14: The Paradox of Medical Progress and Physical Aging 134

Questions of Life and Death • Ever-advancing Medicine • The Deepening Healthcare Quagmire • Medical Miracles—Friend or Foe? • What Have We Created? • It's Not About Ungratefulness

Chapter 15: Challenges to Morality and Ethics— .... 144 Keeping Things in Balance

Ripe Old Age • The Negative Accompanying Medical Advances • A Crumbling Foundation • Disposal Mentality—the Slippery Slope

Chapter 16: Change and Transition 155

Change and Transition Aren't Synonymous • The 3-Parts of the Transition Process

Chapter 17: Personal Identity Assessment (Knowing Who We Are) 161

Knowing our real self • Abstract Personal Identity; Practical Life Activity • Careers Can Mask Our Core Identities • The Anatomy of Career's Influence on Identity • Career—the Benevolent Dictator • Retirement's Missing Link is designed to:

Chapter 18: Enter—Retirement… 171

The Mid-life Nanny Has Also Retired • Vacuum • Finding A Settledness • Is Retirement… • It's All About Youth • A Conspicuous Absence—What's Missing Here? • Production & Youth: the Perfect Marriage

PART II: Aiming Toward Retirement Fulfillment

Chapter 19: Defining Today's Retirement…. 183

It Ain't Our Daddy's Retirement No More! • So What's Going On Here… • Differences between the Old and New Retirement Paradigms • The 'Old' Retirement – Still Available, but Risky • Favorable Odds

Chapter 20: Things Are Different Now 190

Gerontology—It's a Good Thing • Seize the Day! • Looking Inside— Where We Go from Here • Remembering Our Main Intent

Chapter 21: Life Arena #1—Career 199
Career—What to do: • Career—Post-career Options • Five Career Considerations

Chapter 22: Life Arena #2—Family— "The Love Chapter" 206
Family—as applied to retirement • The Truth about Love • The Perfect Retirement Combo: Love, Mutuality, Respect • Care Giving— Determining the Balance • Dependents

Chapter 23: Life Arena #3—Relationships 218
Adaptability

Chapter 24: Life Arena #4—Self 222
Self—Relationship with our Inner Person • Self's Options—for Today's Retiree • Self—Relationship with our Bodies

Chapter 25: Life Arena #5—Spirit 227
Is Spirit Real? • A Difficult Chapter to Write • Developing Positive Appreciation of Spiritual Reality • Why Our Spiritual Reality is So Important • The Consequences of Minimizing Spiritual Realism • The Spiritual Gas Tank • Plant Now; Reap Later • Filling the Spiritual Void • Benefits of Being Spiritually Minded • Spiritual Contrasts; Spiritual Peace

Chapter 26: Life Arena #6—Leisure 243
Paradox of Leisure • Leisure Benefits

Chapter 27: Where To Go From Here 249
Enter: RSP (Retirement Success Profile) • About the RSP

Chapter 28: Epilogue 252
Life's Seasons • Summer's Busyness; Winter's Simplicity

Glossary of Terms and Principles 258

General Book Focus: Retirement Realism

which means—

FITTING THE MISSING LINK OF REALISM TO ITS RIGHTFUL PLACE IN THE RETIREMENT 'CHAIN'

This book explains THREE BROAD CONCEPTS:

1. WHY MOST BOOMERS ARE NOT PREPARED FOR RETIREMENT COMPLEXITY

2. HOW TO GET PERSONALLY PREPARED—

   - gain deep understanding about your total later-life phase, a segment of which just happens to be called—retirement

   - understand aging specifically in relation to retirement

3. STEPS TOWARD A FULFILLING RETIREMENT OUTCOME—Grasping full breadth of the so-called New Retirement paradigm—and making it REALITY in your life—

   - the boomer generation's retirement is dramatically more complex than any preceding generation's, yet offers far more opportunity for genuine fulfillment

   - pre-retirees need to be able to differentiate between the old and new retirement paradigms, then prepare for all the New Retirement has to offer!

YOU ARE ONLY AS STRONG AS YOUR WEAKEST LINK

Common Ground

You and I—and several million others—have a foundation of mutual experience: common ground. We're all boomers; baby-boomers, that is—c.1946-1964 (or thereabouts). We don't know one another but, as are siblings within a family, our niche segment on the line of time is unique and common to only us. No other generation can share the totality of all that we are—together. Even from the days of our youth most all of us understand, share, and feel some of the simplest, sentimental, and serious eventualities that accommodate our generation only:

- simple toys—kaleidoscopes, gyroscopes, magnets and tops
- clothes line clips, cardboard = bike spoke noise
- TV—the magical box introduced that changed the world
- The Lone Ranger, Captain Midnight & Ovaltine®, Our Gang
- Tom & Jerry and 3—Stooges were violent; Elvis was lewd
- parental discipline and respecting authority meant something
- being shocked in high school when a girl got pregnant
- "Where were you when JFK was killed and when NYC went dark?"
- *color* TV in 'every' home!
- the British Invasion / Ed Sullivan
- Viet Nam
- race riots
- men on the moon
- Woodstock—"If it feels good do it!"
- drug culture explodes
- Mrs. Robinson, Clockwork Orange, Love Story
- technology explosion
- Information Age arrives

• values shift; "God is dead.", declining moral excellence
• faster paced society
• political correctness
• a global, shrinking world.

The way we were—and are, today.

Generational bonding—maybe we can call it that. We've all lived through many of the same life events, as does a family....

We—the boomer crowd—have been through it all: *together*. Now, together, we head into the last of life's phases. As we've grown up together, have worked together, we now face retirement and getting old—well, yes—together. This creates an inherent camaraderie among us. It's up to us whether or not we use generational commonality to advantage; we can either isolate and insulate as the years wear on, or we use our common ground in a cohesive, constructive sense.

The boomer family, broadly speaking, can be just that—family. As brothers and sisters within the traditional family find it natural and advantageous to assist and encourage one another, such can be the experience of boomers who consider advantages of, at least, loosely held *community* among the entirety of our advancing generation.

Retirement and getting old are big, complex, wonderful, challenging, difficult, even fearful and dreaded topics. Can it be to *anything* but our mutual advantage to view ourselves in the general sense of helping each other prepare for life's grand finale?

To such end this book is written. No man is an island. There is strength, power, and encouragement in unity; if genuine generational community is underwritten with some selfless love, all the better! I can't imagine any boomer doesn't want to maximize retirement and minimize the effects of its ever-present, ill-associate—aging.

To that end, with you I share many of the blind-spots of retirement and aging I've experienced and have witnessed in others. For instance I've come to find we boomers are presented with the development potential of the so-called New Retirement: retirement life that offers personal fulfillment potential in later years, unheard of in all previous generations. Great reason for anticipation!

3

It's becoming common knowledge that contemporary retirement and aging present situations and challenges far different from those of all previous generations. Our national culture; in fact, our *global* culture possesses a volatility and capacity for rapidly changing unknowns and surprises our parents could only have read about in sci-fi novels, thrillers, and visionaries like George Orwell.

I hope to stimulate your thinking on this subject of life's *grand finale,* pointing your thoughts towards some likely new directions. But *you* will be the decision maker. I can guide, coach, and show you where to look, but you'll have to seek to find.

An important note—

In considering the tone in which this book would be written, I decided a more or less casual, even conversational mode of expression could best convey the personal connection I hope to make with my readers. Please know, however, although the delivery is designed to be informal, the content is highly informational.

The express purpose of this writing is to:

- **present** concrete, factual information *uncommonly available* to the boomer community
- **create** serious thought considering the *whole* of retirement
- **caution** against retirement pitfalls
- **lead** the reader to *confidently establishing* a well-discerned retirement outlook.

Here we are, folks. Society and culture are presenting rapidly changing life paradigms. May we individually grow in truthful, fuller knowledge, transformed into applied wisdom, not relying on societal systems and prevailing cultural influence.

> *To thine own self be true.*
> William Shakespeare

> *Your retirement's up to you.*
> John Lewandoski

PART I

Addressing Retirement Realities

Seeing the Big Picture
Society Doesn't Reveal

1

Don't Get Old!

Ma's Advice on Aging

I can still remember Ma admonishing me about getting old—and smile thinking of the occasion. At the time she was about 85, and I, 50 or so. In her late seventies, Ma (she liked "Mom" but it never seemed to come out that way) had taken up planned residence in a well run, tiered, long-term care village for the elderly.

In her earlier years, my mother believed in preparation and planning ahead. Our lives back then were anything but affluent, but prudent living and preparation, especially after Pop had passed in 1973, became a central theme in her life. Her late life goal was to not be burdensome in any way to my brother and me or to our families, and yet attain as much genuine life satisfaction as possible during the years that would accumulate.

The idea was to *prepare*—later-life care, *with* care—and with as much foresight as possible. In the end, the preparation proved successful. Because of good counsel and sound direction learned earlier on, she was able to set her sights and commitment on what proved to be a good, inwardly prosperous season of later-life.

My wife and I visited Ma regularly, usually on Sunday afternoons. One Sunday Ma asked me to help her get something down from a high shelf in her bedroom closet. She went to reach for it, out of habit I suppose, but grimaced in pain as she tried to lift her arm. (Arthritis and rheumatism had set in.)

Turning to me for help, and in sober humor, she said, "John, don't get old!"

I've tried to take her advice, but I must be missing something....

My mother's physical frame, like an old and worn car, was bit by bit giving way to Old Man Time. Of course this is nothing unusual, but I've never forgotten those words or the advice-giving tone in which they were delivered. We all tend to remember incidents that provoke deep emotional responses. Her physical pain couldn't be relieved; she loved me and was trying to convey both her physical hurt and her concern that before long, I'd be in similar position. As well, she was implying that I needed to be preparing for *my own* aging arrangement, not too far in the future.

The bittersweet flavor of that occurrence, to this day, remains. Every time we'd leave, walking down the hall to the elevator, we'd turn and wave—always wondering if that might be the last gesture of parting love.

Becoming Old; Not Being Old

From many other conversations with Mom, I knew she put a high premium on living fully for as long as possible. She was a realist, however, well understanding the linkage and contrast of a mind that stays sharp along with a body that doesn't.

There is an important concept I want to address here in the book's beginning. If you can grasp the difference between *being* old and *becoming* old, you have a good foundation for being able to sort between preparing for your future and ignoring to do so. Most people don't prepare for *either* retirement or aging, financial security matters aside. People who don't prepare usually 'get old'; those who do prepare become old much more gently. They don't see themselves as "being old", a term associated with what's understood to be a premature, human antique!

So what's the real difference?

Being old means not being mentally prepared for chronological age. With ill-preparedness comes fear and dread, probably our most fundamental of negative emotions. And the spiral circles downward; depression and degrees of despair are not uncommonly associated with such state.

Becoming old is an entirely different arrangement. It is typified not by fear and gloominess, but by overall balance and relative confidence that you have achieved by putting some effort into preparation and planning. Yes, it's all in your head. What you *think* is what you *are*. And if your thinking is backed by a healthy trail of preparation, a relative settledness will be your companion.

This book helps you with that preparation.

The Elderly at Pennswood Village

Mom lived another five years or so. During those years and those regular visits, I got to know some of her friends and contemporaries at Pennswood Village in southeastern Pennsylvania.

It was during that time I came to understand the shifting of personal, emotional perspective among the elderly, brought on exclusively by aging. I came to witness some dramatic life-focus changes that abruptly caused me recognition of what retirement, morphing into old age, really looks like.

Getting to see into the daily lives and shifting thought concentrations of the elderly profoundly intrigued me. It was a mix of interest and compassion; of wanting to know more about how our thought emphases migrate as time goes on, and yet sensing the melancholy sentiment such migration brings.

The more I studied these dear personalities and the life reality they displayed, the more spurred I became to understand

9

later-life in general. Especially with my mother, many an hour could pass discussing mature, newness of *older* life perspective on many-a-younger life experience. Sometimes an elderly friend would be visiting which added to the flavor of the conversation.

The more time I spent with the interesting octogenarians, common traits seemed to emerge that have surprised me. For example, most elders seem to put high premium on *sorting between* the most and least important aspects of life, gravitating specifically toward the former. Things like family and fond memories become very prominent points of discussion, to the exclusion of discussion topics that once seemed to hold more equal interest.

To this day, I have a favorite aunt, now 95, who still lives in the same home she's occupied since 1950. We talk by phone every few months at this point, discussing things that were, each of which appear to take on more direct importance in her world—and my world as well, even at 65, truth be told. Interestingly, thirty years her junior, I notice *myself* becoming more and more an intrinsic part of that life history conversation; shall I say life history conservation! In my sixties, I'm finding my own weeding out is definitely underway. Normal at my age? I know not. How about you? Thresholds vary considerably. I do know now, more than ever, having these conversations with Aunt Martha is much more than simply having a nice chat with a relative. I'm beginning to sense that same importance of roping in things that matter while setting free forever much of the 'everyday' that seemed to once have held such high level of personal fascination and importance.

Overall, aging seems to establish boundaries and limitations in our thinking. It appears that by weeding out what's now viewed as life's clutter, we are more enabled to keenly focus and dwell on things of true meaning and importance, subsequently magnifying aspects of life that endure.

Odd, isn't it, how we don't have this observation during the whirlwind of career life and family rearing! Younger people are caught up with everyday living complexity. Retirees, especially in later retirement (maybe mid-seventies and on), are not. Life, and consequently its focus, becomes pointedly simpler and offers more, well, more *time-centered activity*—categorizing and putting in order what's now become the critically important.

> Although less time remains to live, more time is available to sort through all of life. We'll discuss this paradox and some others in a chapter or two.

The very elderly of today find themselves in a highly complex mix of responses to an unprecedented and rapidly changing culture shift, something totally foreign to previous generations. Genuinely old Americans have, and are, living in two worlds, having experienced a changing life reality of incredible breadth:

> Riding in horse drawn carriages on cobblestone streets and dusty country roads in the first half of the century; watching dust being kicked around on the moon in the second.

Getting Serious About It All

During Mom's last years, I became much more inquisitive of the personal transitions involved in the grand scheme of aging. The more I observed elderly life (to which I obviously wasn't accustomed, being in my fifties), the more was realized how impactful the transition from mid-life to elder living becomes. Also realized at the time was the in-the-face fact before long I'd be facing my own autumnal and winter seasons of life.

Thus began my quest for better understanding retirement, integral aging, and how to best prepare for the ultimate eventuality of both—

becoming old….

Ma left late retirement and genuine old age in August 2001, thankfully making the final journey in her sleep.

Peer Indifference Further Piqued Interest

I don't mean to criticize my mid-life contemporaries with whom I associated ten to twenty years ago. But let me say this. Far more than not, whenever, and for whatever reason I'd enter into later-life discussion with others my age, barely a soul had any interest in later life/aging other than, of course, the usual fare about retirement—finances, fun, forgetting the hassle of job and career. General foresight and preparation wasn't, and still isn't, a concern unless it had to do with money and golden-year-gilded-leisure. This life perspective is, unfortunately, largely the same now, as boomers have matured, as it was in the nineties.

Few my age seem to have much interest in overall retirement/aging preparation; the topic isn't very engaging. As well, not much is written on the topic. So…, pretty much on my own, I decided years ago to at least gain some understanding of life's later riddles I could apply to my own life; possibly helping others as well.

Mom died and I continue to get older (just what she told me not to do!). But I think she'd be glad to know of my continued focus and interest on how the whole later-life eventuality works. All my life I've liked to think, wonder, explore. These are good things, if held in balance with the totality of life realities. I'm thankful to be so inclined. Nevertheless, being a maverick has its limitations. I'm told sometimes, "You *think* too much; loosen up already!"

2

Why You Need This Book

1. To Acquire Missing Personal Retirement Needs which are:

- *First and foremost:* obtaining retirement *truth and perspective.* This means obtaining facts and resultant insight you'll never get from society, and which basically fulfills the book's title—*Retirement's Missing Link.*
- Charting clear direction—what to do with the truth you get.
- Building personal confidence and satisfaction that you are en route to your destination of *fulfilled* retirement!

2. To Learn Balanced Reality for Later Life

- Factoring aging specifically into retirement.
- *Making the two work toward maximization of the total later life experience* which, of course, leads into genuine old age.

3. To Go the Distance

- You are a boxer preparing for a title bout.
- You have a lot to win—fulfilled retirement.
- Your opponent is powerful—aging.
- Your opponent can't think. You can!

Retirement is life's title bout! There is potential for much gain, much loss. You need to be the winner. It's your life finale that will be defined in terms of personal victory or defeat, much of which you can control. Your responsibility is to train (prepare) for the final event, lest you arrive in the ring sloppy, out of shape, and incapable of going the distance.

This book will help you train for all the New Retirement (to be explained) paradigm offers. Society, and the machine-like business entity which mostly runs it, don't know much or give two twits about the difference between old retirement models of previous generations and the new one in which we boomers find ourselves.

Pre-retirees today find themselves in a new retirement opportunity completely unique to the boomer generation (much more on this later in the book). It applies *directly* to you. Are you aware of that? I find most boomers are not.

There is so much good for which to plan! Don't fall into the trap of thinking a simple migration from career to retirement is the stuff of which truly successful retirements are built. Thinking and preparing are involved—just as you've been preparing your investments. Society would have you believe that money and leisure drive retirement, but society is an everyday intangible not in touch with anything that directly affects each of us as individuals. You must think on your own.

The social network, in which all we Americans live, is little more than a non-thinking, ongoing machine of which we all are part. We must not fall lock-step into what society seems to dictate. Unfortunately, the herd usually runs in the wrong direction, following the 'everybody-is-doing-it' mentality. You and I are certainly part of the herd, but need to exercise somewhat of a maverick approach, double-checking where it's headed.

Welcome

If you're a boomer picking up this book due to title interest, you already may have an inquisitive and maybe even strategic line of thinking concerning your retirement phase of life.

Good! I mean that. I've had the same. I've developed a strategic, common sense approach and am helping others do likewise. Join in. It's worth the effort.

This reading invites you to come along with me on a journey I began years ago. I'll share with you where I've been, but more importantly, what I've learned en route to my current retirement experience. You will be more enabled to well adjust to the big change of life just over the horizon. That's the bottom line.

If your outcome is such, my job will have been accomplished in supplying what I believe to be crucial information concerning *the combination* of retirement and aging—information not necessarily popular or readily available—at least in mainstream, pre-retiree circles.

You likely view later life with a mixture of anticipation sprinkled with a dab of fear of the unknown; so what else is new in the course of life! And you're being pro-active about it. Most boomers simply are not—especially most men. Congratulations! It takes some guts and humility to 'ask for directions'—contrary to the silly notion men don't do such things. Pseudo-testosteronal machismo, steeped in pride, if you ask me. Men—grow up, already. Real men (and of course women who already know to do so) seek direction and help, especially when the stakes are large.

Written Mainly for Two Groups of People

Speaking of looking for direction and help, actually it needs to be known upfront that I've written this book with a sense of dual intent. There's a distinction between my two motives.

First, it's designed for:

- folks who are somewhat anxious about upcoming retirement and aging, and who are looking for solutions to the big issues of both. They want to know if there are things they can do that will help them truly prepare for the quantum leap from career to retirement, and for life as the later years accumulate, retirement or not.

Secondly, I've written for:

- the individual who, to some degree, wants to prepare for the next big life phase, but basically is looking for deeper thinking and information than our societal culture provides.

This fact that I'm addressing both groups of people means some of the book's content may seem too deep and technical at times for the person looking just for *how-to* or *tell-me-what-to-do next* checklists. On the other hand, once we get to the last section of the book, such a reader will be presented with 'hands-on' material concerning next steps in preparation for life's great last phase.

In summary, the book is a compilation—

- deeper information on retirement and aging
- "how-to" methodically prepare for later-life (Part II of the book—Life Arenas and the Retirement Success Profile)
- an extensive background of personal insights I've compiled through decades of experience, reading, and training.

So really, there's something here for everybody.

War & Winning

Learn the *war* facts. That's how real military generals strategize for combat. You and I are in combat—with two things:

- Old age and its effects
- A societal culture that perceives
  - getting old as counterproductive
  - retirement as the vehicle that ushers in old age.

Both stand in *direct opposition* to much of *your* retirement success.

Learn the *winning* facts. Then follow up with sincere, targeted, personal planning!

- Get tactically aggressive—now.
- When retirement finally arrives, you will be prepared and readied for *maximizing* what the Golden Years can offer.
- You'll also have acquired information and developed strategy concerning making the best of the aging process.

Gaining Initial Retirement Bearings

- Do you ever take concentrated time to think on the full implications of retirement life?
- Do you have a balanced sense of what retirement is and can be, past the money and the leisure?
- Most of us are usually too busy for much introspection. In other words, living in a state of breakneck pace dims our connection with our true selves, straining genuine connection with who we really are. Give this specific scenario enough decades to intensify, by the time retirement rolls around you may have lost sensitivity to the real John or Mary Retiree, living at: Address Unknown. But this can be remedied.

How much of your day do you simply *function*, without touching the genuine identity of the inner you? By inner you isn't meant a spiritual connection between you and God or your perception of higher power. Rather "inner you" is the *authentic* you that isn't necessarily responsive to your actual life activity, especially during the career life phase. It's the *you* that embodies your hopes, dreams, values, passions, personal goals and more, much of which was established years and years ago.

It's almost as if boomers run on auto-pilot too much of the time, more guided by external circumstances than living in a state of connective sensitivity to what means most to us. Daily life demands obviously must be met, especially in terms of family and livelihood. And because career years are usually immersed in both, the everyday rigors crowd out, or obscure, what may lie—more or less dormant—beneath.

Living up to daily reality demands is realistic, needful, and admirable during career life. But then comes Retirement Day.

Although retirement is far more a process than an event, nevertheless when job demands cease, and unless an alternative career is in the offing, the retiree all of a sudden finds time to think on a more personal level; in other words, our unique sense of personal identity once again is allowed to begin filling in the thought spaces that for possibly decades and decades had been occupied by family and career driven obligations.

A caution flag is offered here: If boomers *wait* until Retirement Day's arrival to begin personal re-discovery they may find, as the Ameriprise and National Institutes of Health data in Chapter 4 indicate, retirement may not be what was expected. The old adage "Don't put off to tomorrow what you can do today" applies.

As we go on in our time together in this book, you'll be able to begin piecing together the complexity that is retirement. Most pre-retirees aren't aware (some *don't want to be* aware) that retirement will involve a lot of rational thought and decision making concerning the blending of personal desires and abilities with ever-present external life demands, including aging.

Retirement also ushers in a specific, usually little-considered but impactful personal *shift of responsibility* of which most pre-retirees aren't aware. The following statement sometimes initially takes folks aback, but makes perfect sense when tied into the retirement transition:

> *You*
> **are now responsible for
> your life management and fulfillment.**

In later chapters this principle of shifting responsibility will be specifically addressed. It's important.

Pre-retirement Angst

Talking personally with many fifties to early sixties-aged boomers, I increasingly find that a degree of personal retirement apprehension centers on:

- a dimming, or at least questionable, economic future
- health issues
- health care availability
- worries about children's/grand-children's futures
- care-giving (aging parents, adult children)
- concern over living longer in a rapidly changing national, even global, environment
- dealing with the effects of aging.

Although we can't eliminate all retirement anxiety, if conscious efforts are taken, the preparing pre-retiree can minimize even the worst effects of retirement life concerns. And that you will have opportunity to do.

Retirement Success Profile— Your Best Wake-up Call

Being a trained and certified consultant, in the latter part of the book I'll be presenting the availability of an in-depth, self-analysis vehicle, the Retirement Success Profile (RSP), which will address very core and personal issues related to your retirement preparation.

This in-depth analysis will not only provide better understanding of retirement complexity, but will specifically help you *fine-tune* a personal life agenda rich in preparatory retirement value.

This wake-up call can be a life-saver in terms of alerting what yet needs to be done, as well as blocking paths currently taken that might be best avoided.

WHAT YOU NEED TO KNOW:

- This book can be a true guide in helping you take in the broader perspectives of retirement and aging largely ignored or simply unavailable from most societal sources.
- Personal retirement guidelines are as important as being trained during adolescence for a career.

Retirement's Missing Link

- Waiting until Retirement Day arrives to begin thinking through retirement is counterproductive.
- As a retiree, you will be responsible for your own life management and fulfillment.
- The RSP (Retirement Success Profile) is the ideal tool to initiate true later-life management. (Much more on the RSP in Part II.)

3

Critical Questions

ADDRESSED IN THIS CHAPTER:

• Questions that help you see how centered you currently are on general later-life focus.

Most boomers, when asked about their thoughts on retirement, especially when the 'aging' word is involved, provide a more or less standard, unenthusiastic response.

Standardization of anything is fine if that standard of measure, and especially in a topic of this importance, is rooted in *truth, knowledge, understanding, and reality.* I often repeat these four words and the real-life connection to them, not to be wordy but because each has deep positive merit if applied, and negative implications if ignored. My conviction is the more you hear these words connected to life patterning, the more positive effect they may have for you.

Broadly, a pre-retiree's response to general retirement questions centers on having leisure time, spending more time on various desires: a little travel, maybe a part-time job, implying *"I can always use a little more money and need to keep busy."* Usually the word aging doesn't arise unless I initiate it. Saying 'keeping busy" is a good way to arrest the specific reference to aging—the topic of considerable disinterest and distaste.

These spoken responses of post-career living are all certainly valid—but lacking. What's missing? In some cases, maybe nothing. During consultations, however, it's usually found that little seriousness and resulting insight concerning retirement and the *concurrent aging link have been considered*:

> *"Yes, I suppose I should be a little more serious in broadening rest-of-my-life preparation, but I really don't know where to begin. Besides that, I don't want to fry my brain over such things. That being the case, I have general plans, but past that, I'll just take life as it comes, I suppose."*

The above actual, pre-retiree quote is a serious, sincere response representative of many boomers. It too often has root in personal, emotional limitations. Unless we must, most of us don't want to go to areas of thought further than we think needed, especially if that path leads to where concepts of uncertainty, difficulty, confusion or unpleasantness reside.

Again, the reality principle kicks in, suggesting we need to exercise nuts and bolts reality in confronting and dealing with life circumstances we don't like. Facing reality, of course, is almost always more difficult than detouring down the path to more pleasurable pursuits. This may lead, unfortunately, to our own ultimate expense.

The road less traveled is the route to take.

Upfront Reality Questions

Pre-retiree interest, obviously and naturally, peers into the common issues of:

- How soon to retire? Enough money? What to do with the time? Can't wait! No, can't retire (money issues)!

When in such discussion, I'll often bring up a question or two to stimulate the discussion away from the customary. Responses are varied; sometimes I get a look of "Say what!?", or "I don't think about those things!", or the all too often blank stare....

On the other hand, some say, "Hmmm. I never thought much about that." That's a good sign, as this, usually, is the beginning of a systematic search in finding more of retirement's missing link.

Below I'll list some sample questions that might get you to think. Run through them, will you, and see if, from the tip of your tongue, you can provide substantive answers from your own current perspective. It may tell you how much past the usual finance/leisure concepts you are, in terms of serious preparation for the totality of later life.

If you have straight-forward, conclusive, solid answers, I don't think you really need this book. If you fumble a little here and there, hang with me as we'll explore and find answers to questions as we proceed.

Each question below pertains to how you perceive yourself currently:

- How much of your personal 'worth' is tied up in your career?
- If you didn't have daily job responsibilities, what would life really be like?
- If I asked, "*Who* are you?"—How would you answer?
- What kind of life challenges do you see in retirement and in aging in general?
- Have you given later life much thought?
- Have you ever had to make perspective shifts on major life issues?
- Do you think retirement will demand seeing some things differently than you do now?
- Who, or what, controls your current life decisions concerning your work, home and social life?
- Who controls your sense of self?
- How much importance do you *currently* put on projected overall health and wellness, come retirement?
- Does the economic downturn impact you causing financial worries you hadn't expected?
  - How will you adjust?
- How do you think your overall life satisfaction level in retirement will compare to what you have now?
  - Better or worse? Why do you think that?
- Where do you find *meaning* now?

- How do you think that will change once retired?
- Are you an adaptable person?
    - Do you think retirement will demand more or less life adaptability?
    - Do you have any current level of commitment to retirement adaptation or simply think you'll deal with it when it gets here?
- Will care giving (older parents or live-at-home grown children) enter into your retirement years? Are you (and spouse) adaptable to such considerations?
- How do you think retirement will affect your relationships with others (friends, new and old)?
- Are you somewhat prepared to deal with ever-encroaching aging?
- After the initial 'honeymoon' (1-2 years) of retirement is over, what will you *really* do with your time?
- *How will it all fit together!?*

So, how'd you do?

I've found most Boomers can't answer with much assurance many of these general questions that impact all pre-retirees. This goes for already-retirees as well.

Getting Started

I don't mean to imply we need all the answers now. That's impossible, anyway, now or later! The idea is to *realize* there are sobering questions that center on retirement life reality which, sooner or later, *will be made evident* in your life; in all our lives. I can tell you from personal experience and from observation of many others, each of these questions are applicable in some regard.

It's a matter of progression, a sequential approach. In pre-retirement, these pointed questions stimulate thinking and get the process of good personal preparation going. Begin now. Start the contemplation process.

Asking difficult questions forces to the forefront life issues currently mostly foreign to our thinking; it reveals something is missing.

I ask you: What *is* it about our culture that influences us to know all about retirement leisure and finance, *but so little about* how we—personally, psychologically, emotionally and spiritually—are prepared for that same event? Why such imbalance?

Our very own society—of which each of us is part—has created the imbalance. So, in actuality, the onus doesn't rest on an intangible society at all, but on each of us individually; it all comes down to who we are, and how we tick in daily reality. We know each of us is a compilation of many influences that make each of us distinct, but isn't it interesting how, as a culture, a society, we seem to all conform to certain traits common to us all. For example, and speaking to the later-life topic:

- We procrastinate, not applying and pushing ourselves with diligence into personal life areas that aren't easy or attractive to approach.
- We all know what we should do, but don't look within ourselves—enough—to realize we've only partial segments of the retirement/aging story. In our defense, I suppose, life's immediate demands overshadow our sense of need for pressing into late life analysis, but we're individually responsible for results, nonetheless.

Summing up, the boomer community lives all too much in a skewed, out of balance thought world relating to life's next phase. My hope is that this reading can be a 'first light', alerting and empowering interest and importance to the post-career dawn soon to break the horizon.

WHAT YOU NEED TO KNOW:

- Confronting yourself with provoking, personal life questions forces a point of reference concerning where you currently are in relation to difficult later-life reality.

- The greater degree to which you genuinely mull over the questions listed, the more likely you will press through for clarity and answers.

- The more clearly you are able to view late-life reality, the better you'll have command in preparing for it, as well as more desire to do so.

- Don't be afraid to get in those later-life trenches, face and grapple with the hard stuff, then emerge *all the better for it!*

- Coupling together both truly being serious about your future with working through the Retirement Success Profile (RSP) are a terrific combination in systematic retirement preparation. The two, essentially, prepare a roadmap most boomers will never own.

4

Reliable Statistics
and What They Mean

ADDRESSED IN THIS CHAPTER:

- Mega-financial management company, Ameriprise Financial, through a detailed national survey study, reveals overall retirement mood among current retirees. Results are more ominous than encouraging.
- Professional financial planners report unmet personal retirement needs of clients are rising dramatically. How are those needs being met?
- Senior Depression—a polluted, rising tide… National Institutes of Health also weighs in.

Ameriprise Financial, the originator of a landmark study whose highlights are detailed and explained below, reveals *current retirement mood* among especially the currently retired. Although the full study reflects what Ameriprise calls a "retirement journey" beginning fifteen years prior to retirement, emphasis by far is centered on the feelings and perspectives of current retirees who've been retired for at least one year to as many as sixteen and more.

The implication of study results is sobering, indicating *far* too many current retirees are finding retirement not to be what they'd expected. The reasons for this are many. Although the retiree respondents of the study are revealing emotional feelings largely based on sagging financial portfolios, much more than money issues almost certainly is suspect.

The study reflects general retiree comments using words such as "happy, fulfilled, sad, worried, bored, feeling empty, depressed." These emotional descriptions seem to well suffice for our purposes.

When *you* are retired, only the first two words—"happy, fulfilled"—will do, right? By the time you and I finish our time together, you'll be in the process of well preparing yourself to *avoid* being a statistic described by the other less attractive emotional sentiments.

AMERIPRISE FINANCIAL Tells It Like It Is

Startling results of this ground-breaking study by Ameriprise *Financial, The New Retirement Mindscape*, 2006, may begin to convince you personal preparation—the sooner the better—for your retirement, and later, is essential if you want to maximize later life fulfillment.

New Retirement Mindscape, 2005/2006

Directly below, the introduction of the study:

The New Retirement Mindscape.^{SM}

A groundbreaking, comprehensive study of the retirement journey.

With significant increases in life expectancy, retirement is lasting longer than ever for Americans. The Ameriprise Financial New Retirement Mindscape study is the first to explore people's attitudes, worries, behaviors, ambitions, and needs in retirement. What should we expect as we begin to approach our retirement years? How will we feel and what will we worry about? How can people prepare emotionally and financially to make each stage of retirement as positive and empowering an experience as possible?

As it turns out, retirement is not a single event. It doesn't take place in a day, or even in a single year. Instead, The New Retirement Mindscape study reveals that people migrate through distinct and predictable stages of retirement—each with its own complex emotions and needs. As people move through these stages, each stage has an impact on every other area of their life—their families, their workplace, their communities, and their financial situation. The Ameriprise New Retirement Mindscape study identified five distinct stages: Imagination, Anticipation, Liberation, Reorientation and Reconciliation."

By
Ameriprise Financial
in conjunction with **Age Wave**
and Ken Dychtwald, Ph.D.
and
Harris Interactive, Inc.
2006

We will concentrate our focus on retiree feedback from two time periods within the study:

1. from Retirement Day to a year, maybe two, thereafter
2. from sixteen years and more after Retirement Day (i.e., seasoned retirees).

The study indicates that nearly *40% of retirees*

"… discover that retirement (during the first couple of years) is often more challenging or just different from what they expected and some complain of depression, worry and boredom." —The New Retirement Mindscape, pg. 3.

Also,

"Lack of planning and preparation likely played a role here. Of all the groups, they are the most likely to say they gave little thought to what they wanted to do in their retirement years."
—The New Retirement Mindscape, pg. 4:
"Worried Strugglers (40%)".

29

Nearly 40%! What this implies, at least in part, is these folks didn't personally prepare for the time of life in which they now find themselves. The study goes on to say that these same "Worried Strugglers" (40% of the study participants)

> "… are more likely to admit being worried (38%), bored (34%) or sad (19%). They have fewer aspirations… and are more likely to feel a sense of emptiness (49%) resulting from a lower work capacity. **Less than a third (31%) say they are greatly enjoying their retirement.**" (my emphasis)
> —The New Retirement Mindscape, pg. 4.

In other words, a whopping 40%, prior to retirement, apparently had no real inclination to prepare their *personal lives* for retirement's major, life-changing demands.

Why no inclination?

- Likely they ignored what they didn't want to confront (prepare now for life's uncertainties later)
- Or didn't see past the money and leisure lop-sidedness of retirement our culture so strongly promotes (to be addressed in Chapter 5).

Speaking of the lop-sidedness concerning money emphasis in pre-retirement thinking, note also from the study what *triggers* retirement *readiness*:

> "The most often cited retirement trigger was a feeling of financial independence or freedom. Survey respondents cited among the top reasons why people seriously think about when, how, and where they will retire is 'when they have achieved financial freedom.' This is the new 'gateway' to retirement."
> —The New Retirement Mindscape, pg. 9.

Conspicuously obvious here is the "retirement trigger" *had nothing to do with anything but money.* This makes matters worse. It reveals the clients don't realize the need for more full preparation than what the financial segment can alone provide. In other words, most of the retirees in the study indicated financial security was their sole criteria for readiness.

Note also the negative correlation between a lone sense of financial security and the 40% of survey respondents who found retirement not to be all that was expected. The study criteria strongly suggest that because retirees hadn't prepared for more than financial security, 40% of them were having a disappointing retirement experience.

New Retirement Mindscape II, 2010

The New Retirement Mindscape study of 2005/2006, cited above, has been updated and, frankly, the outcomes are bleaker than those of that original study.

Below, verbatim, is the Ameriprise Newsroom release dated 9/13/10, approximately five years following the initial survey. (**bold** within the text added for emphasis):

New Retirement Mindscape II^{SM} Study: The Stages of Retirement Have Changed

Tough economic times have had a substantial emotional impact on those approaching and beginning retirement

*Minneapolis—(Sept. 13, 2010)—Americans' attitudes, ambitions and **preparation for retirement have changed dramatically as a result of the recession**. Five years after introducing the stages of retirement, Ameriprise Financial (NYSE: AMP) revisited its groundbreaking New Retirement Mindscape® study to see how consumers' journey to and through retirement has changed. The findings underscore the **substantial emotional impact** the difficult economic environment has had on people, especially those who are approaching retirement or who have retired within the past year...."*

The mentioned "substantial emotional impact" is obviously attributable to clients having difficulty coping with financial loss, resulting in an understandably dimmed sense of excited anticipation they'd hoped retirement would provide.

But it goes past the money issue alone. The impact is *also*

great because all the anticipations of retirement grandeur were hinged on finances. As dollar glitter has faded, it's evident few, if any other support mechanisms are in place to provide emotional steadiness. Had retirees possessed a more balanced appraisal of retirement's entirety, via personal planning and some introspection, dismal financial outcomes could be better taken in stride.

The study results go on to state that *"… in the first year of retirement, a stage once synonymous with feelings of liberation* (from career life), *consumers* (Ameriprise clients) *are facing new doubts, concerns and the reality that **retirement may not be what they expected.**"*

"While the first year of retirement was previously called Liberation (in the original study five years earlier), *the optimism and excitement that once accompanied this stage have been muted by the recession. With sharp declines in the value of portfolios, as well as "forced retirements" due to layoffs and career setbacks, it isn't surprising that people are struggling with the realities of retirement. The decrease in positive feeling is dramatic—compared to 2005, far fewer are enjoying retirement "a great deal (56% vs. 78%), say they are living their dream (45% vs. 68%), or feeling that retirement has worked out as planned (57% vs. 77%).*

And here's the powerful clincher statement from the second study *that directly addresses the case I am making for personal retirement planning.* The study interviewed not only the new retirees (under two years since they retired). It also interviewed other retiree groups based on much longer retirement time spans in relation to "Retirement Day". One of those groups Ameriprise calls the "Reconciliation (16 or more years after retirement") group. These are seasoned retirees who have been retired for going on two decades. Because of such duration, they truly represent experience talking.

Check out the details. They are sobering:

*"Reconciliation (16 or more years after retirement)—While the vast majority of people in the Reconciliation stage continue to feel "happy" (80%), they are experiencing **depression** at a **significantly higher rate than in 2005 (20% vs. 5%).** Troubled by the loss of income and social connections, **they are the least***

likely to say they are enjoying retirement "a great deal" (56% vs. 75% in 2005)."

There are some stark points here:

- The 16-plus year retiree veteran has certainly been through several significant stock market booms and busts in recent years. Retirement Day occurred sometime in the early '90s, a time when markets were roaring and money coffers, compared to today, were brimming. Life, centered around affluence, was good.
- There are deep indicators, however, other than finances at work here. Subtle but powerful, they definitively support the concept that retirement preparation must include grappling with the effects of aging in relation to the retirement phase of life. As the study indicates, these veteran retirees are suffering from *"loss of ... social connections..."* in addition to income loss. "Social connections" covers a lot of territory.

As the ravages of aging increase in later retirement, removed are long-held bonds of friendship, family, and spouses. As is possible, these voids created by such loss need to be somewhat filled with redeeming emotional/psychological replacements. Certainly intimate personal loss can't be replaced, but if sound perspectives and attitudes are genuinely established going into retirement, they can remain the duration and provide guidance and support when life adversity would otherwise usher in severe emotional downturn.

Notice below what the National Institute of Mental Health (part of the National Institutes of Health) says concerning overall senior depression:

NIH Senior Health—on Senior Depression

(from NIH data last reviewed July 2008)

"Of the 35 million Americans age 65 and older, about 2 million suffer from full-blown depression. Another 5

million suffer from less severe forms of the illness. If left untreated, depression can lead to suicide."

"Of the roughly 30,000 suicide deaths in the United States in 2004, adults age 65 and older accounted for about 16 percent of them. In fact, non-Hispanic white **men age 85 and older have the highest suicide rate in the United States.**"

It needs to be noted—

The National Institute of Mental Health aligns with general, professional medical consensus that depression is *not* a normal part of aging. Instead, it's a mental illness brought on by a variety of contributing factors, afflicting all age groups. Unfortunately, aging often produces real-life situations provoking feelings of loss, sadness or grief, all of which put heavy strain on maintaining well-balanced mental vigor.

These numbers and those from Ameriprise concerning depression should at least raise a red flag to readers. Ameriprise data suggests depression is on the increase among retirees that have been retired sixteen years or more. The data also indicates both recent money issues *and* inevitable personal loss are the main contributing factors; certainly understandable.

Turning Negative Data to Positive Advantage

Negative outcome data, as the study reveals, can be a good wake-up call! The *key* to lessening dramatic mental downturns in later years is, in the years beforehand (today would be a perfect time), to *anticipate* squarely the reality of later life's share of adversity instead of ignoring it as many do. "Anticipate" does not mean dwelling upon what may—or may not—be ahead. Anticipation can be a revealer; a motivator. It provides impetus to *establish positive life perspectives* which, in turn, *do* provide considerable degree of counteraction to life's negative when incurred. This can involve:

- developing an honest understanding of our true self's values and passions
- finding our personal and most important life elements and cultivating them
- integrating a spiritual element if not in place already
- resolving relational issues within family and friends as is possible
- focusing on the importance of exercise and good health habits.

This book, overall, is designed to guide and motivate you toward positive, even enthusiastic life initiatives. Balance and stability can be the result.

No Silver Bullet-'Disclaimer'

Neither I nor anyone has a 'formula' or equation for countering the difficulties of later life that easily precipitate debilitating depression. Of course our culture tries glossing over unsettling life reality, padding it with every feel-good fuzzy of life imaginable.

You and I aren't about that here. Instead, we are using common sense, a realistic approach, available information, and worthy, principled planning techniques that combined form advantageous and effectual thinking patterns which can *only* help magnify the luster of later years.

Financial Planners—Essential (but not the whole story)

Three cheers for the professional financial planner!

The Ameriprise study goes on to report that professional financial advisors are increasingly looked to by clients for providing what comes down to personal help for the clients.

Take note:

"Consumers Tell Advisors: Understanding Me is as Important as Return on Investment. Financial advice is

not just about the money. While achieving competitive returns on investments is very important, our survey revealed that having a financial advisor who understands what is important to them (emphasis mine) is equally as important as returns."

—The New Retirement Mindscape, pg. 11.

In due respect to financial advisors, herein lies a caveat. Quality financial advisors (planners) are completely capable of delivering the goods when it comes to investing and financial planning. Unfortunately, it is the rarest financial advisor who is professionally equipped and credentialed to offer substantive retirement life planning advice *in tandem with* that on investing. It appears the Ameriprise study is implying that financial advisors have a professional capacity to *"… understand what's important to them…"* (their clients).

It is true—a sensitive, compassionate, financial professional is a gem to clients when attempting to guide their investment course in the ever-deepening, worrisome quagmire of current economic strategies. But how far can that guidance be expected to travel into personal arenas of life?

Two Different Doctors

Clients, in actuality, are asking for more than is pointed out in the Ameriprise study. Because of both the always challenging investment outlook *and* the potentially formidable societal future in general (to be discussed later), what clients are really asking for is often past the scope of the financial advisor's expertise. In short, the client is intertwining personal worry and uncertainty with the whole of their financial package, dumping it all in the lap of their trustworthy financial guru. Although these two worlds intertwine, they are separate entities that, usually, need handling differently.

Example:

• going to a cardiologist for answers concerning recurring chest pain

• going to a dentist for teeth issues.

Both specialists are needed; one isn't usually involved with the other's expertise.

Another striking implication here is that consumers (clients) are obviously not having their personal life guidance needs met. Reading between the lines, clients are reaching out for real-life personal help in uncertain times.

There's a very telling key phrase in the study that clearly reveals the heart of many clients. They are worried about their money and their personal futures: *"...what's important to them is equally as important as returns."* That statement says volumes concerning the heart-cry of boomers—and current retirees, who are coming to the abrupt realization retirement is far more complex than owning comfortable portfolios.

They want some valid coaching on what to do next with their lives. They've read tons of information on retirement fun, where to live, what to do to keep busy, but are coming up short in real, satisfying, retirement fulfillment should the money engine, which drives so much of it, loses some steam. Of course this is understandable; losing money hurts. But what hurts even more is realizing the void created by investment loss, in addition to other life stresses, can severely crush emotional dreams, leading to depression or worse.

What the study reveals is increasingly nervous clients telling their close financial coaches, "I need help; please, talk to my soul! What am I really going *to do with* what may be the next thirty years on God's green earth?"

The human heart continually seeks peace within it—throughout all aspects and phases of life. Becoming more glaringly obvious in the current pre-retirement phase is money and leisure planning don't fully explain or provide that peace. Frankly, if there's a redeeming quality to the money issues, it provides a stimulus—a wake-up call boomers need in recognizing retirement reality isn't all about what society and culture promote it to be—money and leisure. This will be covered in-depth in future chapters.

Advisors are unrealistically being called upon to be a quasi-information source, able to steer funds, hearts, and minds—

all in one. How many hats can one professional wear considering financial advisors are not licensed or certified personal life consultants?

The conclusion of the original 2006 New Retirement Mindscape study poses a question in form of a clear and highly accurate statement:

"Conclusion: Fulfillment drivers

*So, what is the secret to a fulfilling retirement? Our study demonstrates that retirement fulfillment correlates with a wide range of variables: early financial planning, having a clear vision of retirement goals, continued activity and engagement throughout retirement, financial preparedness, and leveraging professional advice. **As it turns out, money is not what buys happiness in retirement: having a vision for the future and planning for that vision are as important as money in achieving a fulfilling retirement.**"*

—The New Retirement Mindscape, pg. 12.

I respect Ameriprise balance in not only presenting strong, elemental investment precepts but, as well, honestly declaring personal planning is "… as important as money in achieving a fulfilling retirement."

General Summary of Ameriprise Financial's overall study observations:

- Retirement is lasting longer than ever, compounding its complexity.
- There are predictable stages of retirement—each with its own complex emotions and needs. These needs are beginning to have difficulty being met.
- Ambitions and preparation for retirement have changed dramatically as a result of the recession and other factors, resulting in substantial emotional impact.
  - The million-dollar question arises: How can people prepare financially and emotionally?

- Lack of planning and preparation play a significant role in retirement not
- being as expected.
    - Main complaints are:
        - sense of emptiness (49%)
        - worried (38%)
        - bored (34%)
        - sadness (19%)

Only 31% of those surveyed in the 2005 data collection say they are greatly enjoying their retirement. The data collected in 2010 is even more worrisome, obviously connected to the historic market declines in 2008 and the struggling economy.

- Professional financial advisors across the country receive direct, factual, and telling input from clients. The main gist of what they are hearing:
    - "Help *me*, too!"
        - Clients are asking advisors for more than good returns on investments. They clearly are reaching out for personal help in arranging the whole of their lives brought on mainly by the increasing complexity of the economic situation.

[For the written record: I thank Ameriprise for their excellent statistical analysis made public on their website. Every endeavor has been made to transcribe information from their website to here correctly. Their statistics have been used simply to make the point a top-shelf wealth management company, through established public numbers, recognizes the complexity of the retirement dilemma upon us, one to be faced by the just-arriving boomer generation.]

In Conclusion:

What the money management people are seeing and communicating regarding increasing client angst is all true.

From a personal retirement consultant's viewpoint, however, I want to make clear that financial advisors are being bombarded with the *'help me figure out my life'* personal requests, not because clients suddenly see financial advisors as life advisors, but due to gross dips in investment holdings brought on by factors neither the client nor advisor can possibly control. Back in the money bumper crop years—for example, the nineties—clients rarely aired personal gripes because the economy boomed and everyone lived in Happy Town—client and advisor alike.

Point—*the need* for personal retirement preparation, meaning later life preparation outside any type of money issue, *was always there,* but rarely addressed. Today that's beginning to change.

In general, unless tough life eventualities grab retiree attention, preparing for how life is to be handled as aging increases is usually either an oblivious concept, or ignored through ongoing procrastination. As is typical of human nature, when money coffers are full, "life is good" becomes the main mantra; preparation for anything more than investment comfort plays a distant second fiddle.

This personal preparation need, that's always been there but rarely voiced, is well illustrated in the above Ameriprise statistics. (I'll repeat the data here.) The study's seasoned retirees—sixteen years or longer—are just now reporting grossly increased incidence of depression:

> *"Reconciliation (16 or more years after retirement)— While the vast majority of people in the Reconciliation stage continue to feel "happy" (80%), they are experiencing* **depression** *at a* **significantly higher rate than in 2005 (20% vs. 5%).** *Troubled by the loss of income and social connections, they are the least likely to say they are enjoying retirement "a great deal" (56% vs. 75% in 2005)."*

Would these folks, sixteen or more years ago, be less depressed today had they prepped for a retirement far more complex than a growing investment portfolio? I don't know. I do know, however, that boomers with whom I've shared retirement complexity and have helped sift through personal goals, values, and possible life directions emerge steadied, fortified, and confident in grabbing all the gusto the so-called New Retirement (Chapter 18) offers. Investments are only one piece of the retirement pie.

"Money isn't everything" is a hackneyed term, I realize. But the phrase is so weighty in actual fact that it can't, really, be overstated—especially in a boomer culture that, for the most part, has been *centrally built upon* money and its materialistic outcomes.

I *don't* mean to degrade a balanced approach to materialism and pleasure. Only to point out that the baby boomer generation, because of various converging factors that will later be addressed, finds itself consumed with the pocketbook. This is said not to place blame nor criticize, but to merely state the way things are.

Get Certified!

One last word on CERTIFIED FINANCIAL PLANNER™ Professionals (CFP):

Get one!

"Certified" is a designation that only comes via intense education, examination, and experience. Financial planners are ubiquitous and may or may not be well-schooled. This is not to say non-certified financial planners can't give you excellent service. It is to say, however, that the certified planner has proof of considerable financial education and training from which you should certainly benefit. Look for the word "certified" and the trademark symbol.

You almost can't afford *not* to make the small investment. These financial professionals are the reciprocal of the Certified Retirement Consultant (what I do).

The former guides by means of historical financial data, current activity, and projected financial trends; the latter helps navigate through life's more personal maze, having your best later-*life* plan at heart. Because my son-in-law is a Certified Financial Planner™ Professional, I've seen, firsthand, applied financial skills result in considerable easing of the mind, especially in the current financial climate. Knowing him as well as

I do, you probably presume me biased. To a point that's true, but I've sincerely come to realize that a good financial planner truly does have the general welfare of the client at heart as much as I do. We just come at that goal from different directions—same desired result: a happy and content client!

It's Not Just Ameriprise Financial

Ameriprise Financial is not alone in helping their financial advisors grapple with what's actually an emotional overload heaped upon them by pre-retiree clients. All money management companies, in fact, are seeing the same thing: pre-retirement boomers and actual retirees trying to make a positive go of later life amid current investment strains, some losses, and an ever changing and challenging financial climate.

Bank of America/Merrill Lynch Wealth Management, an international powerhouse, has garnered information from a varied panel of top experts who touch the retirement arena in one way or another. In an online presentation series, Merrill Lynch reveals general retirement sentiment findings that, expectedly, parallel those of Ameriprise Financial. Because Merrill Lynch has assembled a diverse panel of experts, the combination of insights provides an exceptional cross-section of contemporary retirement perspective. You might want to tune in to the panel discussion. Probably the simplest way is to Google "help2retire merrill lynch".

I've personally been in discussion with several top-level management heads of these major money management service providers, finding general consensus among them: Today's retirement landscape is nothing like that of previous generations.

WHAT YOU NEED TO KNOW:

- The face of retirement is in major paradigm shift.

- An unexpected source—the most sophisticated financial/wealth management firms in the *world*—well understand the personal issues boomers are facing concerning retirement.

- Possible investment deterioration, living longer, and health care are major concerns to the majority of pre-retirees.

- It's becoming increasingly evident personal retirement preparation is as crucial as financial planning, maybe more so.

- You don't want to be one of the negative statistics major retiree studies are revealing.

- You *can* help yourself.

5

Lopsided Reality

ADDRESSED IN THIS CHAPTER:

- Our culture offers developmental education and personal guidance for mothers-to-be, children, adolescents, young adults, newlyweds, and certainly those in career preparation—*why none for the retiree*?
- Genuine later-life aversion issues—why we have them.
- Is personal retirement preparation worthwhile or a waste of time?

Current Retirement Thinking

Broadly speaking, are these among the main topics you consider when thinking about retirement?

1. having enough money
2. finally get to relax
3. keeping busy
4. trying to stay healthy

Going a little deeper, how do you answer these questions?

- Outside the 60 Plus Association, AARP, Modern Maturity and like organizations that provide general guidance information to the retirement/aging segment, how are you personally being guided (or plan to be) into transitioning from career life to what's next, be it an encore career, simply headed toward what we've always known traditional retirement to be, or something in between?

- Even more fundamentally, do you in fact think
  guidance and personal preparation for the career to
  retirement transition is really *that* necessary? (Some
  boomers do not.)
- Do you feel our societal culture at large particularly
  focuses on the future well-being of the *individual* retiree?
  Asked another way:
  - What's the last *'Personal Retirement Preparation'*
    class you've attended at your local Junior College,
    for example…? (Get the point?)

We all understand ubiquitous money management and leisure planning information abounds. Retirement-related *personal* education, however, is virtually non-existent within our
culture mostly because *retirement isn't seen as a cultural, value-
added commodity.*

Instead—retirement, from a highly *impersonal* societal perspective, is quietly perceived as more a societal burden than
anything else. We live in a society where *producing*, mainly in
terms of general business and commodity climates, is of central importance. Retirement and aging—understandably—and
within that production mentality, are not viewed as producers.

Consider:

- Retirement's classic definition. Basically, it implies with-
  drawing from producing (career life) to relative relaxation—retiring from the career phase. This flies in the
  face of anything even related to production mentality,
  the concept which keeps society in perpetual motion.
- The Gross National Product, outside specifically selling
  goods and services to the retirement community, isn't
  increased by relaxation!
- Old isn't physically desirable, pretty or sexy.
- The whole of later life points in only one direction—increased physical and, usually, mental frailty ushering in
  the end.

Senior-oriented organizations, as mentioned above, provide
nominal personal retirement attention, but their general approaches are directed toward mass retirement consumption,

not at all toward the individual. Many government and health-care agencies address basic senior needs but, as well, don't hone in on individual 'how-to' training that could aggressively aim and propel pre or actual retirees toward positive retirement objectives. I'm not saying there should be such a program. It's simply the way things are.

Realistically, retirement is a name given to a limited segment of a much larger reality: *later-life*. And to spell it out, what motivation do the young or hard-working mid-lifers have to concentrate on older people who have 'already lived' life? Outside selfless compassion, not much.

These are facts of life and, whether right or wrong, somewhat explain why life preparation for seniors isn't exactly a societal priority! Of course this also implies society isn't head-over-heels enthused about personal, emotional growth development for the "over the hill" gang. How our culture perceives retirement is understandable—but not helpful to the individual.

If later life/retirement education and support *are* desired, and society doesn't provide it, individuals must obtain it on their own. But...

Do individual boomers want help? Do they even think they need it? Increasingly, a reserved affirmative answers both questions. Frankly, however, most pre-retirees are blasé about personal preparation, at least until they see the larger panorama of retirement complexity—and the negatives of later-life in others compounding the problem.

Later-life Aversions

There's really no mature way around avoiding realities of later life we don't like. Fact of the matter, of course—as time advances the weld between retirement, old age, frailty and death strengthens. Sorry. Just the facts.

Many boomers seem indifferent and lack a true-grit retirement preparatory attitude. Even amid the joys and anticipations of what's perceived as actual retirement, many understandably have what manifests as a sometimes nearly debilitating aversion to the negative aspects of later-life reality—in short, a usually unspoken fear of the withering outward frame of mankind: increasing illness, frailty, and general system deterioration, death. Any *wonder* there's aversion!? To deal with the aversions, the whole of later-life is sometimes tarnished and often at least back-burner relegated. In other words, the thinking goes something like this: "When it all gets here, I'll deal with it."

So we have the bad combination of an out-of-touch society along with indifference, fear, aversion, and procrastination resident in some of the boomer camp. The combination leads to an uniformed, mid-life career person heading into the biggest transition of their life, only to be greeted by the abrupt reality results of ill-preparation.

Indifference and procrastination are more easily dealt with than the aversion to aging difficulty. I can tell you this, however: Although aging and death are inevitable negative life outcomes, if our perspective about them is infused with broad, positive, late-life reality—of which there is considerable—the aversion is held in check. Preparing, through learning, is one of the main keys that unlocks the door of satisfying later-life, beginning with the retirement stage.

Why We Avoid the Unlovely

In the '60s, the unfortunate pop culture mantra was "If it feels good, do it." Back then—when we were young…, nobody *thought* 'retirement'. It seemed as far away as the moon; something for old people.

Fast-forward to today: a pre-retirement mantra should be "*Even if* it *doesn't* feel good, *do it anyway!*"

Psychology indicates our psyche tends to disassociate thoughts, words and concepts that have little or nothing to do with what makes us feel good: a defense mechanism of sorts.

- *Pleasure Principle:* the seeking of pleasure and avoidance of pain makes us feel good, but often overshadows the Reality Principle.
- *Reality Principle:* meaning that instead of always trying to skirt, suppress, put off, and avoid issues we don't like—which inherently lack pleasure—we maturely address and grapple with these, head-on! (Ever wonder where the current buzz phrase: "*Deal* with it!" came from?)

To many people, the words *retiring, aging,* and *death* just don't go well together. We usually don't want to acknowledge such linkage. You may wonder why link the three terms together at all. Answer: *realism*—a life-trench realism we'd as soon ignore. But can't.

Here's the usual rationale: *retirement* is going be great; *aging* is no fun at all; *death*—well, the thought of it is usually left to funeral occasions and happening to somebody else, or "Just change the topic—I don't want to talk about it." Although we can jest or joke about death or ignore it entirely, we all know it—and the strains of life the lead to it—are as integral to retirement and aging as salt is to the ocean.

Human nature tends to skirt this reality linkage even though this potentially painful end-time connection is in-our-face obvious.

Can you see wisdom in preparing *now,* to avoid rude awakening and confrontation in time to come? Preparation *alleviates* painful aversions.

I realize many readers aren't at all squeamish about discussion of the retirement/aging/death triangle being integral to later-life reality. Some actually invite working through the concept for a variety of reasons. But—experience has shown me how amazingly high the percentage of boomers is who, really, just don't want to 'go there'.

We can't prevent what we know is likely inevitable, and no one wants to spend any time on the morbid. I realize we all know this, but pose the point here as it challenges us squarely to question how much *other,* even lesser life reality, is avoided just because it's unpleasant. Think on that. Later-life isn't like teeth: if you ignore teeth, they go away.

What to Do

1. *Begin to strategize your personal defense* against negative that can severely tarnish your coming retirement. Side with your good sense against deceptive thinking that tells you to put off later-life prep! Taking positive steps will not only provide satisfaction in accomplishment, but moreover, an assurance you are doing what's right. This means anxiety will be lessened because you've confronted aversions you don't want to face.

   You also have a starter tool in your hands. In a few chapters ahead, you'll grasp insight that will make the puzzle of the retirement/aging connection more clear—the better you understand the enigma that is life, the better you'll be able to much more clearly plan your way through it. This understanding is another facet of the "missing link" in the retirement chain (book title.) Chapters center on:

   • aging's complexity
   • aging's positives! (believe it or not…)
   • how to make good decisions on these tough life issues, and more.

2. Strongly consider using the Retirement Success Profile, to be thoroughly explained in Part II, when you've completed the book to reveal your current, overall, retirement preparation status, and structure later-life direction that really does fit who *you* are. It forms a personal baseline, centering on each area your life touches: career, family, relationships, self, spirit and leisure.

   Every person has life blind spots that are easily missed. The RSP brings these to your attention so you, with my analytical and consulting help, not only can plan out your strategy of addressing life's best possible direction, but likely even reveal resolving blind spots now, before age slams them in your face, unannounced.

Why All This *Negative* Focus...

Because there's too much indifference, procrastination, and aversion that prevents boomers from *tackling* themselves! Yes, that can be done. The pre-retiree needs to *take down* that part of self that follows the societal herd of narrow retirement thinking.

Most everything I've written in this chapter so far has a negative connection to it. I don't like it, either. Remember— this book is about *realism*, which by definition presents conditions as they actually are; not idealized with Hollywood touches and feel-good fuzzies. I'm all for positive, too—and we'll get there.

For now, determine what group (below) most accurately describes your fit. By categorizing yourself, you may be prompted to look more closely at where you currently stand in your approach to retirement perspectives:

I find there are broadly three groups of boomers when categorizing them by how they view later life:

- You, my reader, are likely in *Group A*. You take the whole of retirement seriously and are learning all you can about it. You are doing precisely what our culture will not do for you—getting past shallow glitz, what sells, and what appeals to little more than superficial perceptions of weighty issues.
- The bulk of boomers, however, fall into what I call mainline pre-retirees. These folks comprise *Group B*. They can be characterized by taking retirement at face value, seeing it largely as their parent's saw theirs, and have little awareness or concern over major shifts that are changing the face of retirement. They realize there's good and bad in every life stage, live mostly for today, and are content to see what retirement is all about when it gets here.
- Then, there's *Group C*. Sometimes I'm confronted by skeptical boomers who, initially at least, interpret all this preparatory stuff I advocate as superfluous and negatively focused. Even though they readily acknowledge retirement life can involve some major changes (they usually

can't or won't enumerate many, if any, by name), they view taking personal preparation seriously as a waste of time. In addition, I've been told all I do is dwell on the negative; I'm "Chicken Little" and the retirement sky is about to fall.

I find *Group C* boomers usually to be characterized as having so far lived life on-the-edge, in the fast lane, and often not willing to sit still long enough to grasp the entirety of preparation discussion leading to later-life maximization. What sometimes seems to be a one-way monologue can go like this:

*"Who **cares** about what could happen later on! Why should I go looking for trials or trouble! Let them find me!"*

*"Why can't we just forget the negatives of later-life? After all, we know they are part of life; **we'll just take what comes and deal with it when it does.***

(I can be assailed as well): *Let's talk about the good! Why not reinforce all the advantages of retirement, Mr. Consultant? Tell me more about some neat, new ways I can spend the money I've saved all these years. Tell me more about new fun ways to spend my days. Show me avenues of new, creative retirement enjoyment that somebody hasn't already written about."*

When the barrage is over and the big picture realized, usually such skepticism abates. I agree there's certainly merit in not putting any unneeded focus on negative. But preparation for its potential occurrence is another story. That story is as positive as can be:

Good prep is about applying positive approaches to what we understand to be potentially negative reality.

There's a difference between positive thinking and ignoring things we don't like. Being positive and accentuating what we like is certainly good and productive, but it can lead to our detriment if we conveniently ignore its counterpart, the unpleasant. Life realism must operate in reasonable balance.

The question, therefore, is *how* and to *what degree* we balance things we'd just as soon ignore but can't. And just how do you gain the criteria that helps enable such solutions to transpire?

If you Google "retirement", you'll find absolutely no shortage of how-to books centered on retirement leisure, financial planning, where to live, and how-to enjoy yourself. Much, if not most of it, is good and applicable. There are also many insightful books on the aspects of aging.

But there's a chasm of thought falling between the joys of retirement and the difficulties of aging associated with it.

Most boomers anticipate the joys of retirement *and* the eventual effects of aging, but usually don't see the connection of the two traveling on parallel tracks, so to speak. Cognitively, all this is surely understood, but preoccupation with the Pleasure Principle can easily overshadow the reality that lies underneath. The beauty of realistically viewing long-term retirement joys *and* ills—on the same level plane—can motivate insightful boomers to get past the traditional retirement/ aging, black & white narrowness that's so commonplace.

If the Ameriprise study (Chapter 4) is examined between the lines, The New Retirement Mindscape subtly reveals that when the good-life (Pleasure Principle) is altered due to the props of secure investment being pulled, or even only shaken, many retirees have little emotional grit and reserve to withstand the fallout—

Is there a missing component here?

At least part of what's missing is that the bulk of media and print concerning retirement doesn't address life's reality trenches, leaving boomers with an *imbalanced* and highly incomplete evaluation of later-life. If retirement were as kick-back-simple and dual-sided (leisure & finance) as society implies it to be—

I wouldn't need to write—and you wouldn't need to read— this book!

WHAT YOU NEED TO KNOW:

- Our societal culture puts virtually no emphasis on your personal retirement preparation. You must make things happen.

- Boomers tend to shy away from, and put off, facing later-life reality, dwelling instead only on aspects of it that are pleasing (Reality Principle vs. Pleasure Principle).

- Pre-retirement is the time to begin strategizing your personal defense against that part of you that will procrastinate. Side with your good sense against deceptive thinking that tells you to put off later-life preparation, or rationalize away that very need.

6

Feelings—
and the Need for Truth

ADDRESSED IN THIS CHAPTER:

• Our retirement overview is too often based on half-truths, opinion, and feelings.
• Fickle feelings can't replace sound truth.

Did you notice in the previous chapter that most of the focal points there revolve around how people feel concerning a variety of issues?

- Society, for example, *feels* the getting older scenario counters that for which a strong society stands: producing. This sentiment isn't broadcasted that way, but unquestionably that's the feeling drift.
- Secondly, the Pleasure Principle is rooted in nothing *but* feelings.
- And then we looked at three groups of boomers who are jam-packed with feelings about how later-life is generally viewed.

Feelings are extremely powerful. They, ironically, are also one of the most delicate and fickle of our faculties, being easily steered by influence and circumstance.

Aiming our feeling-focus on retirement, if I were to ask you what your emotions and responses are when you focus on retirement, what would your answer be? For example, do your feelings reflect

- deep worry or concern
- uncertainty or skepticism
- a mix of the above
- don't really think about it
- not much of anything—"Hey, life's too busy now to think about retirement. Got all I can handle right now!"
- desire to know more in case I'm missing something
- want to be prepared for retirement, best I can
- anticipation and can't wait attitude
- tell me more!

Whatever your current sentiment, it's a compilation of multiple life input from all your life sources collected over the years: your interaction of experience with all of life—people, places, things, circumstances and experiences. All these lumped together in your thinking now provide your current overall feeling-picture of life's next stage. Your current observations, unless they change, will define what action you will continue to take, or not take, in dealing with your own retirement and later-life.

What has led you to read this book? Whatever you now think of retirement—plus/minus, good/bad—has resulted in reading the book in your hands, correct? You do have a purpose, wanting to know more.

Because you have purpose in acquiring more information, this presents other questions:

- Why, in the first place, do you have a *void* that spurs you into this further inquiry?
- What's missing that creates that need?
- What, or who, hasn't delivered?
  - Is it your culture, surroundings, environment?
  - Is it your own fault through previous laziness or indifference?

In my discussions, I generally find that boomers most often don't put nearly high enough premium on personal retirement preparation and, consequently, don't take the time to get serious about it all. Not that they haven't good intentions, but like getting the yearly physical or teeth cleaned, it's simply put off.

We almost always find time to do what we really want to do.

Why are you reading this when so many of your contemporaries wouldn't give one twit of interest or concern? You *must* have come to the conclusion that at least some additional sober investigation into late life reality is simply prudent and smart. I couldn't agree more.

Feelings, Emotions and Truth

I began in the section above by asking what you currently *feel* and how you emote when thinking to life ahead of you. "Fickle feelings", which are the internal expression of an emotion, can easily deceive, distorting truth. Our actions are too easily the result of what our emotions tell us to do. Somehow, the three: mind, feelings, emotions are intrinsically bound and need to be checked against rational thinking. Conscience and value systems also play into the equation. We'll touch on these, too, later in the book.

Certainly we should and do trust many feelings. We do so because we trust the origins of what has been the initiate of those feelings. As example, we feel positive that a heavy oak chair in sound condition will easily support our weight. We do so because that feeling is based on *truth;* i.e., *facts we've gained* from long-term experience in sitting, the strength of oak, and the craftsmanship reliabilities of chair makers.

Retirement, obviously, offers no long-term experience from which to draw. There are some facts we know about retirement, but are those fact sources sound, unbiased and reliable? Are they rooted in what we know, with as little question possible, to be *true*?

What we are coming down to is first determining truth from falsehood and, second, complete from incomplete.

This concerns our retirement or anything in life that demands some sort of decision making. It is when we possess *truth* that we possess the key of assurance in whatever it is we pursue. When we have truth, *reality* has arrived. It may not be reality upon which we cast a favorable eye, necessarily, but it's genuine. We can make good decisions based on truthful reality, whereas it's impossible to do so when our thinking can only count on shifting questionability.

Truth and reality nicely grease the rails of life, don't they; why don't we pursue them more! If we can reside in the stability of truth, we don't live in a continual place of uneasiness and question, doubt, concern, or worry.

Truth: *a bad word to ever be underused; a good word for all times*; the bed-rock of reality. We're not talking about truth versus lies here, but rather truth in its rawest essence. Truth— anytime, on any topic—balances every-*thing*! Truth is the ultimate determiner of *what is*; what is not. It separates fact from fancy. That's why it's the essence of reality.

Truth also separates light from darkness. If, for example, one is blind and is only familiar with what those with sight know to be total darkness, and all of a sudden sight is granted, obviously light is apparent. Reality is achieved; *the light has revealed a truth* to the blind person indicating an illuminated world exists that, earlier, wasn't even conceived as being real.

If reality is truth, the key is to get our hands on enough of it that we are benefitted! The goal here, when you're done this reading, is to sense something akin to the assurance you may have had when finished listening to the venerable, now deceased, Paul Harvey. Remember the endings to his radio broadcasts: *"And now you have the **rest** of the story. Good day"!* Mr. Harvey would fill the missing, factual information of a story on which you'd originally possibly had only sketchy information. What a satisfying feeling! America had come to trust Paul Harvey. He delivered reality once he had the factual truth.

I'm not saying anyone is fully truthful or is full of only the truth; we all are obviously fallible, but Paul Harvey was a friendly voice that could be trusted. Retirement linked with aging is not a topic that touches the heart and soul as did Paul Harvey interest stories! But—if you can grasp the rest of the story of later-life—the balanced truth and perspective of it, past the elusiveness of fun and money—think how broadened and clearer your forward gaze can be.

Truth Gets Things in Order

Obtaining as full measure truth as possible has a wonderful way of eliminating mind clutter and confusion. Although truth isn't necessarily pleasant, possessing it can lessen fears and unwarranted life aversions, and all but eliminate nagging questioning. All this is freeing and enabling. *We need to know what we believe and why we believe it*, all of which contributes greatly to far more balanced sense of emotional and cognitive confidence.

By taking the time and effort to seriously seek out overall retirement truth, and getting past society's not providing it, we are in good position of being prepared for later life eventualities *regardless* of what may arrive. It's better to have and not need, than to need and not have—my paraphrase of what I learned as a young Scout.

I still carry a sturdy knife for various utility most everywhere I go. Thanks, Mom, for taking me to all those Scout meetings after school....

We Can Be Our Own Problem

Society skews truth and distorts reality. We've all been conditioned by our culture *not* to see the rest of the (retirement) story. But not everything can be blamed on the world around us. Retirement reality can be distorted by ourselves if we, indirectly maybe, purposely sidestep truth we don't want to address.

Let's face it: A lot of reason the not-so-fun aspects of retirement and later years don't make our thought headlines is *due to our own emotional makeup of avoiding the unlovely* touched on in the last chapter. I don't mean to open a nasty can of worms here, and don't take these comments personally. We are all pretty much the same, including me.

Let the truth be told: If we lack in full truth and knowledge, because of our own ineptitude, laziness and excuses, we ultimately *short* ourselves, standing in our own way. Although societal culture shorts us too, as you'll see in the next chapter, suffice to say we can be responsible for creating our own fuzzy-view of the years that await us.

WHAT YOU NEED TO KNOW:

- Truth: a bad word to ever be underused; a good word for all times. Seeking truth is worth every baby-step or hurdle because…when we have truth, *reality* has arrived.
- *Reality is seizing the rest of the story of later-life*—the balanced truth and perspective of it, past the elusiveness of leisure, fun and money.
- Be convinced that getting the big picture of your retirement is to your considerable benefit. Thus, be motivated!

7

Social Pathology and Big Business— Bad Combination

ADDRESSED IN THIS CHAPTER:

• Be assured—no segment of society will provide personal, strategic, retirement life development planning for you. Preparedness for your individual retirement well-being is *yours* to develop.

• America's ongoing move away from traditionally strong and moral societal structure affects every segment of life, including business, and ultimately even affects retirement and aging.

Boomers—a Spoiled Generation?

Baby boomers (Americans born between 1946-1964) have been brought up in a societal culture that has been strongly driven by technological explosion, a generally strong resultant business climate, and individual relative wealth never experienced in any preceding American generation. It's also a generation that largely exalts money, materialism and *success*—however the term be defined.

The post WW II baby-boomer generation has been a *recipient* generation—receiving what parents never dreamed a possibility during their lives. Parents, who had foraged to keep livelihoods

60

afloat in the early 20th century, knew first-hand what deprivation meant. By mid century, many a loving parent, after the Great Depression and war experiences, and with industrialization in America gaining great traction, set sights on providing their children the so-called 'better' life they themselves didn't have. And thus was born "The American Dream".

Along with well-intentioned parents came hyper-advanced technology. From arguably the '60s on, the unprecedented information and technology powerhouse has been making America a virtual volcano of material production and unending accumulation. This, coupled with a bestowing parental wish to supply more than they had had, catapulted the youth of mainly the '60s and '70s to be a generation that would assume brand new societal paradigms their parents had never experienced or imagined.

The Boomer Generation is an *enormous* (head-count) generation with more opportunity, freedom, education, longer life, money and the ability to achieve long-lasting success—than any which have preceded it! Welcome: The Boomer Generation.

Much—very much—can be said, debated, and argued about whether or not these major societal changes have been, and continue to be, a blessing or curse. Likely, the result is a mixture. We won't cover that debate here other than to address something upon which we likely can all agree. And that is this—the statement: *sickness is a curse.*

Sick Boomers?

Unfortunately, a 'disease', if you will, has infected much of the Boomer Generation. I call it Social Pathology. This dressed up term has been around for some time under various titles: Social Disorganization, Applied Sociology, Social Problems, and Practical Sociology.

"Although the terms have variations in shades of meaning, they are commonly used as synonyms."

—Social Pathology, p. 429, Edwin H. Sutherland ©
    1945 The University of Chicago Press.

Social pathology is a real entity affecting, and *infecting*, humankind. It usually relates to what are perceived as societal negatives such as poverty, old age or crime, all of which tend to increase social disorganization and create personal maladjustment.

Does all this mean boomers, as a generation, have 'social problems'? Well, pathology means functionally deviating from what we know as normal. In other words if a group of persons (boomers) aren't functioning in a way American culture traditionally has known to be normal, in that capacity it could be considered, well, sick. Will you stay with me on this?

With all the boomer generation has going for it, an insidious 'infection' prevails most Boomers don't even recognize! How can there be sickness, with symptoms, and not know it!? Even more ironically, the illness has something to do with *success*, the same word used in the first paragraph above. Screwy, isn't it? How can *success* be sick? Am I saying *a component of the boomer generation is **successfully** sick?* Yep. Sorta....

The sickness logic presented here centers around a generation that has *deviated from (pathology)* what our American culture has, for generation upon generation, understood to be the broad definition of success: *success: favorable or desired outcome* (Merriam-Webster Dictionary).

General American tradition, until the '60s, had seen success to be an admirable goal. Although admirability has always depended on personal values, past generations have commonly understood success to be end goals successfully attained through honest work endeavors, application of sound principles such as the Judeo-Christian ethic, having a strong family, and being well esteemed by others because of admirable life demonstration of one sort or the other. Wealth could be, but not at all necessarily was, a measure of success.

With the arrival of the '60s and on, however, the old ideology of success changed. What was once a more honorable progression of goal achieving transformed into a me-first, body-climbing scramble to gain 'the moon', all too often regardless of principle.

I can remember in the late '60s, just starting out in the business world, witnessing a ruthlessness of personal advancement

I'd never known at home, school, or in the community. It seemed the goal of many of my generational peers was to body-climb to the top—doing whatever it would take to get ahead.

Social Pathology and Big Business— Bad Combination

As goes the heart of a generation, so follows what it constructs and worships. What the boomer generation has constructed is the enormously productive and successful American industry that has been the envy of the entire world. This industrialization, in turn, has contributed to the creation of what could be called a secular object of worship—money and materialism. In other words, relative wealth, if not carefully restrained by sound personal conviction, becomes a new doctrine exalting comfort and pleasure as the highest goals and values. It replaces time-honored, disciplined sensibilities with an inordinate pre-occupation and untamed desire that at one time would have been understood as living "over the top", to put the idea in the vernacular.

Industry, of course, is abstractly neutral, needful, and if used correctly becomes the infrastructural backbone of a nation:

1. Man creates things—industry
2. industry creates jobs
3. jobs create money
4. money enables purchases
5. purchases deplete inventory which then perpetuates the cycle.

Although American industrialization began pre-boomer, the last half of the century became the rocket ship—a catalyst, really—that innocently yet insidiously supercharged and lured boomers away from traditionality into a new age. And it's been definitively called "progress". (I'm reporting the story; you make the ethics call....) Indeed, in some ways progress is exactly what's occurred, but in other ways, pathology (sickness) may be the more appropriate word.

Greed and pre-occupation with satisfying self: the bane of mankind—combined with weakening of sound principle in the process—can destroy a nation, even a people. The Roman Empire is a classic example, and dare I suggest America, as of the 2010 decade, needs to sharply take notice of its own teetering value judgments.

The Boomer Generation, not by intentional design but by slowly deviating from long-held traditional value, has opened the door to imbalance within the society it's created. The entire preoccupation with being driven to success and to having more, and more, and even *more* materialism has created imbalance in even the way the current boomer generation approaches—*retirement*.

The Retirement 'Industry'

The dilemma is this: Because boomers have become firmly conditioned to acquiring all the materialism possible during the mid-life career years, *that same mindset transfers into retirement.* A money management expert recently said to me the general slogan that characterizes many clients, and is often actually stated by clients as well as peers, is

"I earned it. Now it's my time to spend it!"

Although the comment is true, it clearly depicts where retirement emphasis dwells—on wealth and what it buys—or in one word: *materialism*—the doctrine that comfort, pleasure, and wealth are the only or highest goals or values (Webster's New World Collegiate Dictionary.)

As business is all about supplying goods and services that meet demand, is it any wonder even the specific retirement industry (meaning all business that focuses on retirees and seniors) is the monstrosity it is? Demand for goods and services, certainly among the 10,000 boomers that are 'retiring' every *day*, has never been higher. This is not to say the enormity of the retirement industry is at all to be devalued, nor are we, the boomers, who demand the supply it produces. In fact, as indicated above, constructive industry is a welcome addition in building and maintaining economic soundness.

Our economic structure, from which we demand supply, and big business that supplies it, aren't a negative issue. Problems develop, however, as people put *excessive value* on all that's produced and consumed.

"Excessive value" is obviously subjective. I'm certainly not establishing guidelines for any individual, but am judging the entire concept along these lines:

When values of leisure, things, and wealth (materialism) exceed deeper, more fundamental life values, possibilities for developing imbalanced emotional outcomes increase. (Case in point: the depression statistics in the Ameriprise study *The New Mindscape*, Chapter 4. The study revealed when money coffers decrease among current retirees, the incidence of major depression dramatically increases.) Ironically, such imbalance can result in more difficult, personal life outcomes than the lessening of materialism alone could ever impose. In short: it ain't all about the money. I see it all the time.

Fuller pre-retiree reality perception and balance is lacking because *money and leisure currently form the main pillars of successful retirement value,* instead of deeper life values which more involve personal fulfillment.

General boomer perception of retirement is, therefore, truly based on half-truths and partial information. "The rest of the story" is lost in all the glitz.

Because the boomer population is so immense, its purchasing power is practically orgasmic in the mind of every CEO whose company offers a product or service that strokes this booming generation's wallet. The goal of the retirement industry is, of course, to drive its products straight into the all-too-eager arms and hearts of the largest generation of spenders ever to inhabit the planet.

The Retirement Sales Message

The sales message the retirement industry sends to its consumers is delivered through superlative marketing techniques. For fun, let's look at a few:

- Smiling, fully silver-haired, beaming faces of always good-looking boomer models, presented in any and all merchandising venues reveal a happy and prosperous retirement experience. Their full heads of vitamin-nourished hair and mouths full of gleaming white, perfect teeth exude all the wonder retirement can be! Wow! The Golden Years *have* arrived!
- Ads for vitamins and supplements for older men/women show happy couples on ocean liners, bikes, in kayaks, dancing, frolicking with grandchildren, all because they are 'fortified' with this or that contemporary snake oil.
- Every evening nightly news-based programming provides ads, *ad nauseum,* offering availability of wonderful supplements, methods, or cures for 'active' retirees.
- As many boomers eat supper around boob-tube daily events, many of which are enough to give you gas, we take a bite of good food only to be comforted by an ad for eliminating gas! No gas? How about diarrhea? No? You're stopped up? Well, we have something for *that, too.* How's your esophagus? Did you tell your doctor *all about* your esophagus?" Dry eyes? Allergies? Gotcha covered! Peein' too much? No? Okay…. Peein' not enough? Oh, sure. We've got stuff for that bulging prostate causing nightly trips to the potty—you'll pee like a *kid* again! *Wait! Don't change the channel!* Are you peein' in your pants? We have catch-all pee-pads, *too!*
- Then, just about as supper is done, our doting, gerontological guardians present the ultimate delight: a nightcap ad guaranteeing erections for "…when the time is right", complete with a *we care about you* disclaimer lovingly advising that erections of 4-hours or longer (I wish!) are problematic and that blindness and hearing loss are possible, along with other minor side effects. (Ripley wouldn't believe this stuff!)

Oh, they care so much. The business world is surely helping us with our retirement security, even in our bedrooms. All I can say is: *Thank God for the DVR and its fast-forward function!* Although the stuff we see on everyday TV targeting boomers can be funny and we poke a little humor at it, the mega-retirement industry isn't problematic. I've been in and around major business all my adult life and have admiration and respect for marketing techniques originating in creative minds.

Marketing is neutral and interesting, for the most part. Where the damage is done is on the receiving end; it's this *diet* of relatively unimportant, consumed-with-me well- being and pleasure seeking that is gloating the gut of pre-retirees. It's like eating at the local yummy doughnut hangout every day, sucking in such delicious wasteland food, but having no regard whatsoever as to the need for fruits and veggies!

If society, business, and our culture at large produces retirement thinking mostly related to self-satisfying money and leisure, are not boomers being shorted on balanced input that would, otherwise, provide better real-life decision making and emotional well-being in their own future?

Most of the cultural input that shapes our thinking, feelings, and determination of our conclusions on how we view the coming retirement phase of life is lop-sided information (Chapter 6). In many conversations I unfortunately find that the average pre-retiree relies heavily on society's retirement norm for defining their later years. Much of this imbalance occurs simply because no one has informed them otherwise.

WHAT YOU NEED TO KNOW:

INFLUENCES

If boomers are influenced strongly (and they are) by society's general perception of retirement, those influences strongly shape how we feel about and approach later life.

Societal influence originates in three weighty, cultural concepts:

1. the high premium placed on money
2. leisure fulfillment
3. a shifting, ill-defined, understanding of current retirement structure.

FEELINGS

Following influences, feelings develop. If we rely mainly on feelings to shape retirement life perspectives, those perspectives may not be rooted in strong, thought-thru rationale.

PERSPECTIVES/DECISIONS

Perspectives are usually what direct decision making. Here it all gets crucial because decision making is directly related to actions and real-life outcomes.

OUTCOMES

Outcomes are the fallout—good or bad—that result from decisions made.

Note the progression above:

1. Influences—be careful of your source of influence in all things
2. Feelings—practice separating sober rationale from what you feel
3. Perspective/Decisions—pray or meditate over the often conflicting mix of feelings and what seems logical
4. Outcomes and follow-through—commit to the decisions made.

- Even before we get further in this book, examine your current thinking on retirement and aging. In a quiet time, actually define these things within and apply them directly to yourself.
- What kind of mind picture does that create for you?
- What decisions, if any, have you drawn to help your inner person prepare for life's last major stage?
- Are those decisions based on feelings, solid information, or both? Or neither? Do you really have strong later-life commitments at all?
- Do you see the need to adjust, or even develop, some current perspective on life direction?
- If so, don't be afraid to reframe perspectives; it's like putting a valuable print in a new picture frame.
- Be brutally truthful with yourself. Tell your mind to not rely on what you feel, but to what your inner voice bears witness as truth.
- Remember, obtaining truth is your aim. Truth will reveal reality, and that's where we all do best to dwell.

A few additional ideas for thought...
- Consider what has most influenced many of your major decisions in life.

- How do you define personal success?
- Ask yourself how important materialism will be in your retirement.

T.A.R.—a Miry Mix

Chapters #8, 9, 10, and 11 center on the inextricable mix of

> **T**ime
> **A**ging
> **R**etirement

The next four chapters form a more specialized 'technical' grouping than the others. I mention this here so that as you read through these chapters, you know the balance of the book won't be as abstract as the *combination* of these three concepts—time, aging, and retirement demands in these chapters.

Time, aging, and especially the later-life stage of retirement together form a figuratively poignant sticky 'compound', you might say. This is probably because retirement forces to our thinking the reality of life's last phase. And life's last phase easily raises issues of time and aging. And thus the *miry mix…*

Think of water. Water can be experienced as a liquid, gas, or solid. But all the forms of water, though different from one another, form the basic compound of hydrogen and oxygen we know and experience water to be. So it is with T.A.R.

The chapters aren't all that dry…Wait till you read the excerpt from the Mayo Clinic! Talk about a later-life miry mix!

8

Time, Aging and Retirement: Inextricably Connected

ADDRESSED IN THIS CHAPTER:

- Time is profound because—
  - we humans can't possibly influence it in any way
  - it affects absolutely everyone
  - it's so subtle in its progression we never see it.
- Retirement brings the element of time and aging into more sharp focus than ever before.

In its simplest analysis, aging exists only *because of* time. The human retirement phase, obviously, falls under the jurisdiction of both time and aging. Regardless of how we might categorize these elements of life, the older we get, the more we sense being stuck in, and with, time's advance. (A deeper look at "The Complexity of Aging" in Chapter 10.)

Time and aging are two abstract realities that directly influence, but can't control, our life reality. In other words, although we can't alter the immovable beginning/ending life boundaries, we do have control, to large extent, over what happens within them by intelligently responding to their influence. We can't move the boundaries, but we can well navigate within them, if we so choose.

Brief Thoughts on Time and Aging

Not that it's a life imperative certainly, but in a sense of wonder, have you ever given the passage of time and its relation to your own aging some thought?

Aging is one of those features of life that is

- so powerful we humans can't possibly influence it in any way
- so profound it affects absolutely everyone
- so subtle in its progression we never see it. Like the wind, it progresses at its own invisible pace. We know not from where it originates or where it goes. As wind in the trees, in fact we only know it to be real because we see its effects.

Aging reminds me of the sun's course across the sky. Morning wakens and all creation greets the dawn. Morning presses afternoon, which appears, but soon yields to the setting sun, often clothed in melancholic hue—before the night does so appear. And then it repeats itself, again and again.

It is said man is granted three score and ten (70 years); 25,550 days, if we do the math. Minutes, days, months, quickly compound into years. Have you said to someone recently, "Seems the older I get the faster time flies"?

Aging is as obvious to us all as is a passing day. Unless we conscientiously stop to think on either, both pass virtually unnoticed, yet continually accumulating. Every so often, life jolts us into the reality time *is* hurrying on: "Where *has* the time gone?"

The passage of time equates to aging. Profoundly simple; invisible, yet surrounds and transports us continually.

Critical Focus in Retirement

Our retirement phase of life has a way of putting aging into critical focus, usually in relatively short order. Prior to mid-life, generally, our lives are like a camera lens that is in soft focus—focused enough to render a picture but not much more. We aren't concerned about sharp, critical focus. We live day to day not giving much thought to the passage of time because we are too busy living in it.

As age advances, it's as if the lens *snaps* sharply into crisp focus—alas, very real are the wrinkles, sags, aches and pains, and all the other baggage aging drags in tow. But it goes much past the physical experiences of life.

We begin to see, have more respect for, and even sometimes loathe time's passage. Time has ushered in a sharp focus we sense all too clearly!

No Time for Aging

We may not have time for aging, but aging has time for us! Time is no respecter of *any* person or any *thing*. It relentlessly bears upon all Creation, sparing nothing within its advance.

A remembered instance illustrates humankind's vulnerability to the timeline of life. Twenty to thirty years ago a very prosperous, mid-life businessman and I were engaged in a discussion about business growth and expansion. At one point, somehow the discussion focused on retirement. The gentleman actually owned several businesses at the time and considered further expansion. Impressed with such zeal, I remember asking specifically whether or not he thought he'd *ever* retire. He replied in the negative, but somehow the word *aging* was carried into the discussion, probably on the back of the word retirement.

The engaging conversation halted. . . I'd inadvertently hit on a part of this fellow's soul that tripped a not uncommon trigger. With a smirk, he exclaimed, "Keep that aging *so & so* away from me. I'm not goin' *there!*"

In an "I hear ya" kind of alliance, I remember agreeing. We

both dropped the subject and got on with business. Back then, in early middle age, neither of us appreciated talk about—aging! Funny, though, aging has never relented despite our unchanging sentiment toward it.

What this man *said*, for the most part, is what most of us *feel*. Who of us wants to hang around, or even spend time considering, a late life entity named "Aging"—whose first cousins are known as ailments, uncertainty, personal loss, physical loss, retreat, withdrawal, solitude, depression, and last but not least, a really *nasty* cousin, Grimsley Reaper, aka the "Clean-Up Man", I like to call him—the dude with black hooded cape, no face, reaping scythe…. A splendid personage is this "Aging", don't you think?

This crew of highly experienced 'bad guys' is left over from the Fall of Man, who have not only existed since then, but wreak havoc in everyone's later life to some degree at one time or another. Not welcome *anytime*, we can bet they'll show up *sometime*; during old age (over 75 or so), young-old age (up to 75), and even during a time we hope to be wearing our life's crown jewel—the anticipated Golden Years. How *dare* this happen!

The truth:

Retirement is unfortunately in bed with old age. An oddly-coupled set of bedfellows. If only we could position our retirements in a less adverse and hostile time slot of life! But when, alas, would that be?

Time Delivers Both Life and Death

Later on we will explore how *transition and change* (Chapter 16), though different from one another, facilitate major shifts in life experience. Time, itself, however, has some interesting properties that work both to our advantage and disadvantage.

For example, as career life ends, retirement begins.

If we arbitrarily look at our lives in broad terms of thirds, they can be distinguished as

- birth up to the career years (childhood and educational preparation)

- career years to retirement
- retirement years into old age and death.

As soon as we are born, aging begins and we start to die—sobering, isn't it. Not negative thought, just reality. Life, therefore, as related to time, deals with descents and ascents. Just as we descend (die) to one stage, we ascend (are born) to another. We depart one and arrive at the next.

Here are three brief examples of this ongoing birth/death, birth/death continuum that greatly impress me. They may you, as well:

- The *seed/reproduction cycle:* kernels of corn, for example. If a kernel of sweet corn is planted and given the right natural conditions, it will die unto itself. For a reason. That death will bring forth exceeding new life in the form of an enormity of new kernels. In kind, it's been said man counts the seeds in an apple—but God counts the apples in a seed. I love that one…, the wonder of life.
- The *seasons:* without the passing of each, the succeeding cannot follow.
- *Insect metamorphosis:* the lowly worm must give way if the butterfly is to emerge.

"Don't get old." Mom had said. What does that really mean? Corn seeds become old and die and profoundly reproduce in their dying. One season gives its yield only to usher in the next.

WHAT YOU NEED TO KNOW:

- We can ignore time and aging, but they won't go away.
- Time is integral to and affects everything we know as life.
- Dealing with time is a lifelong human exercise of transitioning from one life phase to the next.
- We can't control time and aging, but can control how we respond to it.
- We respond best if we understand the human relationship to time itself. The understanding of our place in time isn't complex, but it is paradoxical. Chapter 9 will attempt to unravel it a bit, to our advantage.

9

The Paradox of
Retirement and Aging

ADDRESSED IN THIS CHAPTER:

- What's the difference between being old and not being so? How can you tell?
- Retirement is two-faced!
- So is society!
- Time is not on your side, but you can make the most of it.

A paradox is a weird sort of thing. What else can contradict itself and seem absurd but, in another way, express something entirely believable. I think of Paul Simon's song title "The Sounds of Silence" (1966). By common definition, silence is the absence of sound, but set in a different context within our thinking, silence can 'speak' volumes, as this song's title and lyrics so profoundly express.

Aging, and retirement linked to it, is chocked full of such paradox, ambiguity, and relativity. *Why is this important to know?*

The broader our view of the whole of life, the more that understanding can be incorporated into *forming more balanced and insightful overall life perspective we can use practically, everyday.*

Paradox is commonplace in life and isn't as theoretical and complex as it sounds. For example, here's a short questioning statement, illustrative of my own life. It involves *paradox*, the double-forked tongue of *ambiguity*, and how these concepts intertwine, making them *relative*:

"I'm 65 years young—eh..., old? Wait a minute...! Which am I—young or old?"

Paradox: The phrase "I am 65 years young" is like saying silence is noisy.

Ambiguity: We can be young from one person's perspective, yet from another's, old. Which is correct—at 65, are we old *or* young? (In this case, the ambiguity is also relative.)

Relativity: Where, on the timeline of life, is the distinction made between aging and not aging? Even though we *age from birth,* is a 2-year old considered to be aging?

Who's older: Jack LaLanne, the fitness guru, who exercised daily nearly up to his death at age 96, or John Q. American—fat and half-ill from stress and lack of activity at age 55 or 60?

How we *perceive age* is very important, for how we feel and think subsequently dictates how we act. And, largely, how we act is the real determiner of how 'old' we are.

Retirement is as paradoxical as aging and, of course, both relate to each other, deepening the puzzle. The new freedoms retirement brings are wonderful, providing relative simplicity of life away from the workplace, even some solitude when and if we want it.

But on the other hand, losses are beginning to occur: longtime friends begin to pass away, good health is more difficult to maintain, and the solitude we once so longed to be able to experience may prove to be more curse than blessing.

Overall, the paradox of aging frees us from one thing, but binds us to another. We have lots of life experience, but as retirement lengthens, much less time and ability to use it.

In the chapters ahead, we won't find solutions to these almost mystical quandaries of living life, and certainly not the Fountain of Youth that could prevent all the confusion! But in an overall sense, by the time you've completed this read, it should be evident that we don't have to live in a paradoxical mess of aging. We learn not to live *in* the puzzle of life, but to *respond to* it positively, in as fulfilling and fruitful ways as possible.

The Big Umbrella

Part of the book's main theme is about learning the process of delivering quality adaptation to the difficulties of later life, for our own good and that of others. I say "learning the process" because conditioning ourselves to pursue positives, in face of a continual negative—aging—isn't easy; it takes resolute effort and resolve that will, however, offer reward.

Some seem to have a more natural proclivity in grappling with the unfriendly elements of later-life than others, but all struggle. The aging foe is a tough one.

We've already acknowledged that integrating the reality of the aging phenomenon into our society's general retirement theme isn't much explored or at all popular. Aging 'doesn't sell'. Also, our pleasure-principled thinking naturally avoids— or ignores—the unpleasant.

All the more need, therefore—the need to better understand the whole of retirement, which includes the complexity of aging.

The better we understand the retirement/aging relationship, the better our chances of maximizing later-life fulfillment.

Truthfully solid, acquired life information, understood, enables us to draw rational, sound judgments and conclusions. Such a base provides development of good perspective that can then help guide us in beneficial cognitive reasoning and decision-making; again—all toward *maximizing* later-life fulfillment.

The way it is:

Retirement neatly snuggles with its bedfellow, aging. In fact, it's really a sub-set of aging.

Aging is like a big umbrella under which retirement happens to fall.

It's important to note that our last, *major life phase*—we call it retirement—is certainly not the curtain call of life. Although it falls at the end time period of lifespan along with aging's complications, it nonetheless remains in its own category of *personal development*—a time of potential and personal blossoming impossible in earlier life stages. This isn't pie-in-the-sky dreamland. In chapters ahead we'll uncover that even aging can deliver inward, developmental capacity unattainable in earlier years.

All to say—retirement is good; aging complicates. Can we reconcile the two? The answer is yes, to large degree. It depends on perspective, attitude, personal decision making, and stick-to-it commitment.

Retirement: Paradise or Paradox— Making Sense of It All

Paradise: An *invalid* assessment of not having to work and being in command of our later years.

Paradox: A valid, but potentially troubling, joyful anticipation of post-career living *starkly offset by* the problem of diminishing time and energy to enjoy it.

The paradox works like this:

Retirement is downright two-faced—it says one thing but does another. On the one hand it offers a well-deserved respite, garnished with life-long accumulation of experience, and likely some wisdom thrown in to tie it all together. One would think this arrangement of having time to now spend on what we want, based on a lifetime of living experience, to be an indisputable win-win. In other words, we've gotten life together now and, finally, have the time to put it to good use! With career life responsibilities being behind us, some money in the bank, and available time we've never had, we could almost term retirement "Heaven on earth"; paradise, relatively speaking.

Almost…

Then the sober twist:

Paradoxically, our life timeline has been largely *used up* in previous decades and is increasingly diminishing. We have more free time, but progressively less and less *real* time to enjoy it! Pretty blunt stuff, isn't it. Almost seems like a gyp-job: ripped off; something like growing too soon old and too late smart, or somehow missing the proverbial boat.

79

I realize what I've just said, of course, isn't earth-shattering news; we all know we get older, retire and die. But—the ultimate point of this entire writing is *we can do something*—cognitively, volitionally, emotionally, spiritually, and physically in confronting the unfriendliness of aging. We can't beat it, but we can respond sensibly and strongly, *dampening its effect* on our retirement period. The last part of the book will provide clarity and expand this considerably.

Societal Culture Fuels the Paradox

Time working against us isn't the only issue in this retirement paradox. The society/retirement link is another strange bedfellow arrangement delivering boomers a further negative and sobering twist.

Society, like retirement, also *says one thing but delivers another!* It masks and distorts retirement reality, emphasizing the glitz and leisure while glossing over, or being oblivious to and ignorant of, much more important considerations of retirement life such as establishing strong, realistic later life purpose. In reality, society's retirement message is somewhat ignorantly deceptive because it doesn't come through with the rest of the story. It only concentrates on business, leisure, kick-back rest and fun of it all. Here's some of what it misses:

- **quality of life emphasis**
- **purpose and goal development**
- **constructive fulfillment**
- **familial and relational harmony**
- **spiritual balance**

Frankly—society's take on what retirement is *can age people prematurely,* because matters of the heart and individual well-being simply aren't considered. "There oughta be a *law…!*"

Do I need to tell you this ires 'n' fires me up in what I trust is valid indignation and because of my inability to *fix it?*

One day I was so steamed about this short-changing of the boomer community—*in addition to* the difficulties of aging—I had to blow off some exasperation. Poetry is less lethal than fury:

Retirement's Personal Paradox

Multiplied years; more wisdom gained.
Compounded decades; less time remains.

Our culture commends, "Press to the hilt!"
But is this the basis upon which is built

a retirement of bliss—the late crown of life?
Or tagging along do seasons of strife

in parallel glide, sight-unseen?
Such enigma perplexes; can concord we glean?

©2009 John Lewandoski

I wrote that in 2009. Since that time, this book has gotten underway, and I've found the paradox of retirement and aging to have mellowed somewhat. Most likely that's due to more intense thought and reason applied—I'm putting into practice what I preach in this book!

How Shall We Then Live?

You already know this but it bears repeating: Retirement and aging are unfortunate bedfellows. Each is resident within every life if we live long enough. *Each of us are responsible for* increasing the joys and fulfillment of retirement and, in so doing, decrease and offset the aging lamentation.

Two paradoxes stand out in later-life:

1. The retirement phase itself is paradoxical as it ties in with aging. Retirement offers us a life free of career and, usually, family demands. If we've at all prepared for retirement, we have some idea of what will provide fulfillment in it. So, just as we arrive with lots of time

on our hands, we encounter increased speed of the life time-clock. Bluntly, just when work is done, we notice a dead-line ahead. Get my drift?

2. Secondly, our culture, the media, and big business appear to be pro later-life, but in actuality don't at all support it on a heart or individual level. Retirees (and certainly the genuinely aged) 'produce' virtually nothing that can be measured in dollars and output, which leaves societal support and perception of post-career life as being weak and dim. Another dead-loss for retirees.

Given this puzzle of later life which can't be reversed, *how shall we then live?*

• We have basically two options:

1. Sit around and see what life brings along.

2. Be proactive by getting good focus on later-life's *attributes,* shifting self into gear, and then heading where that focus leads.
    • Step out of life negative that feeds on itself. Just as negative feeds itself, likewise does the positive.
    • Be observant.
    • Look keenly.
    • Think concretely and positively.

• What should your general goals be?
    • quality of life emphasis
    • purpose and goal development
    • constructive fulfillment
    • familial and relational harmony
    • spiritual balance

WHAT YOU NEED TO KNOW:

• We can't understand some of life's puzzles even if we stand on our heads in attempt.

• On the other hand, some of what seem to be unanswerable life enigmas aren't that at all. Instead they are more cloudy areas of thinking than completely unanswerable queries.

- Sometimes all that's needed to understand the seeming unanswerable is to apply some initiative—in other words, seek and you will find. Clarity can result.

- Build a strong foundation to support later-year uncertainties through knowledge and subsequent preparation. If you do, it's better than money in the bank, and you will have found that retirement link most boomers don't even know, or acknowledge, as missing.

- We don't have to live in a paradoxical *mess* of aging. We learn not to live *in* the puzzle of life, but to *respond to* it positively, in as fulfilling and fruitful ways as possible.

10

The Complexity
of Time and Aging
(For the More Technically
or Theologically Inclined)

ADDRESSED IN THIS CHAPTER:

- A look at some theories of the entity of time itself
- Preparation and discipline—keys to managing the aging concept
- Varied personal belief origins influence how we perceive the whole of aging.
- Is aging necessarily bad or evil?
- Controversy reigns concerning why we age.

In previous chapters, we've seen how retirement, time, and aging somehow all interrelate. Much of that interrelationship is puzzling, paradoxical and, likely, past finding out in its entirety, at least from mankind's corner of the universe.

You know? If we didn't know the need to take life seriously at times, we could almost acquiesce to dumping the whole 'consideration of time' into a funny, funny riddle pail—and be done with it! In fact that's what most do. And that's not to be faulted. On the other hand, some of us find interest in trying to determine how it all fits together.

The whole of time, motion, space and matter, especially as

related to human birth, aging, and death, is so staggering to contemplate, many simply don't. Who among us, however, in contemplative moments, cannot be awe-struck at the absolute wonder of how it all hangs together.

Trying to grasp—even a little—of the conceptual, invisible reality of time is staggering. Will you meander with me just a bit through the time/aging concept, because of the wonder of it all, if for no other reason? For the purpose of our study together, though, I'm touching on this area for more than just the wonder of it all. We will bring together *the combined relevancy of:*

- *birth*
- *time*
- *aging/retirement*
- *death*

that such attention may help us to better come face to face with everyday living—for the long haul. (I haven't said this is easy; only necessary.)

The more we understand our relationship to reality, the better we adjust to and live within it.

Some readers may be technically inclined and appreciate digging under the surface of abstract ideas. If you are such, you know that there is virtually no end of theory and controversy as to what time, mass, and motion—all of which are intrinsic to aging—really are and how they relate to one another.

Most of us just live and move within the dynamics of time and, like the air we breathe, time is to be used, experienced or, if necessary, even endured; not figured out.

Nevertheless, if you have interest in a broader understanding of time conceptualization, a cruise through the two following public website articles is enough to stimulate the most lethargic cerebrum! Have at it!

Both articles are printed verbatim—the first, just a snippet; the second, only the introduction, both because of length and depth. Each, however, can be researched fully online, if desired, providing a superb, mental-gymnastic workout!

The first article:

New Theory of Time Rattles Halls of Science
By Robert Roy Britt
Senior Science Writer
posted: 06:22 am ET
06 August 2003

> *A radical new theory of time and motion has some of the world's physicists doubting the claim while others laud the 27-year-old college dropout who came up with it, an unknown big thinker named Peter Lynds.*

> *Lynds says he's no Einstein. In fact, he is not a fully trained theorist. He has no real academic credentials. But he does appear to have a new career, now that one other theorist compared his work to the groundbreaking ideas of Albert Einstein.*

> *In a paper published in the August issue of Foundations of Physics Letters, Lynds claims to see time and motion with unprecedented theoretical clarity.*

> *Lynds refutes an assumption dating back 2,500 years, that time can be thought of in physical, definable quantities. In essence, scientists have long assumed that motion can be considered in frozen moments, or instants, even as time flows on…*

> *…While we await a verdict on the possible genius or hubris of Peter Lynds, perhaps the rest of us can get on with striving for our own goals armed with a new expectation of actually reaching them, even if we don't quite understand why. http://www.space.com/scienceastronomy/time_theory_030806.html*

The second article:

The Experience and Perception of Time

> *First published Mon Aug 28, 2000; substantive revision Tue Nov 17, 2009*

> *We see colours, hear sounds and feel textures. Some aspects of the world, it seems, are perceived through a particular*

sense. Others, like shape, are perceived through more than one sense. But what sense or senses do we use when perceiving time? It is certainly not associated with one particular sense. In fact, it seems odd to say that we see, hear or touch time passing. And indeed, even if all our senses were prevented from functioning for a while, we could still notice the passing of time through the changing pattern of our thought. Perhaps, then, we have a special faculty, distinct from the five senses, for detecting time. Or perhaps, as seems more likely, we notice time through perception of other things. But how?

Time perception raises a number of intriguing puzzles, including what it means to say we perceive time. In this article, we shall explore the various processes through which we are made aware of time, and which influence the way we think time really is. Inevitably, we shall be concerned with the psychology of time perception, but the purpose of the article is to draw out the philosophical issues, and in particular whether and how aspects of our experience can be accommodated within certain metaphysical theories concerning the nature of time and causation.

- *What is 'the perception of time'?*
- *Kinds of temporal experience*
- *Duration*
- *The specious present*
- *Past, present and the passage of time*
- *Time order*
- *The metaphysics of time perception*
- *Bibliography*
- *Other Internet Resources*
- *Related Entries*

Please go to the website for further research on the individual topics, above. http://plato.stanford.edu/entries/time-experience/

What we all really need to know about time is an awareness of its impact on our lives to the point we are motivated to determine our best means of dealing with time's super-sorry end effect we know as progressive aging.

Aging! We can get angry with, frustrated over, languish about all its effects—such actions only adding in futility to rightly perceived negativity.

Instead, we need to realistically, not whimsically or in fantasy, gain basic understanding of its characteristics. *Characteristics of aging aren't the same thing as the effects it causes.* For example, one of aging's characteristics is simply the advancement of time—something neutral. We can't fault that.

The broad concept of human aging's characteristics actually holds some benefit, even though the physical and mental effects command no such respectability. Some actual benefits of aging will be discussed in the next chapter.

Reshape—now!

As pre-retirees, we can now learn to begin to shape—reshape, if necessary—our deeper, inward thought patterns and convictions of retirement-related aging, *before* we get to retirement. In so doing, and when applied later, our thinking will have already been made ready to embrace the new paradigm of life's next phase, which will certainly include experiencing life in a new application. We will be able to more directly dive into retirement life reality, *productively*, from the get-go.

Giving thought now (planning) not only prepares, but conditions us toward retirement adaptability. Because retirement will usher in life changes, is it not better to somewhat flex our adaptability muscles *before* we arrive? Adaptability now can mean more resilience to change when we arrive. (Note, that's *resilience,* not resistance.)

In Part II we will touch on the trait of adaptability. Because retirement adjustments will likely occur in areas of how we perceive life satisfaction at that time, the greater our sense of ability to adapt to such changes, the better the adjustment.

Work while it is day and you have the light to see, for when night comes, the light will have been extinguished.

Planning and thinking ahead is good sense to most people. Our fault usually lies in the putting off of either or both.

Avoiding Back Trouble

'Disclaimer' of sorts: unprofessional but experiential advice!

All this preparedness reminds me of the two back surgeries for disc herniations I've undergone since 1998:

Had I planned ahead; if only!

Back in the day, in my teens through thirties, it was oh, so easy to ignore/put off good planning for later back care. First, I had no one to provide information on caring for the back, nor knew of such need. Secondly, I must admit, I wouldn't have listened had the information been available to me. Had I learned—and applied—back stretching and strengthening technique along with the body-building, the lifting of 150-pound white oak hunks of firewood-to-be (from a bent over position, no less), likely the anguish of later life crawling to the bathroom would have been averted.

"We grow too soon old; too late smart."
(Pennsylvania Dutch saying)

Ignorance, abuse, neglect, and indifference comprise an*other set of sick-sisters* (like retirement and aging), and can often endure for a season.

Tell me: who of us, before the pain hits, thinks much about care of the 'girdle' of muscles that encases our mid-section— meaning the front, sides and back muscles, all of which work together in keeping the bending and lifting functions in good, pain-free operation. Not many do.

Although the abs get a lot of 'six-pack' notoriety; the obliques some, all because sloppy-looking side muscles detract from body symmetry; it's those poor, ignored, lower back muscles, which impress no one, that are a center of neglect. It's true. Who among us does on-the-floor exercises *specifically* for the lower back? (I do—now!)

It is not until lower back pain exceeds the pain of performing exercises and good body mechanics, that we'll do those things!

89

Discipline Thine Self!

Prepare now; think ahead; say "no" to the laziness of self: *The retirement you save may be your own!*

Remember those upfront reality questions back in Chapter 3? Several, if not most, questioned *how well prepared,* in general, you are for living out daily retirement life and beyond. What they directly address is your *current, personal perspective* on those important life issues listed. As you answered, were there any voids in response? Likely there were; if so, that's okay. They'll be filled as we go on. But have you thought of any of the questions, in seriousness, since you read them? Is there something inside telling you, "I really *do* need to take these issues seriously."

Also, be mindful of the Ameriprise study analysis on retirement (and implied aging) found at the end of Chapter 4, which summarized retirement and aging are far more complex than most anticipate or realize.

Keep in mind not to only be thinking of your retirement phase of life, but for the unrelenting aging years that both accompany and increasingly follow. We understand the difference between retirement and aging, of course, but it's easy to miss or lose the efficacy of the combination of the two in tandem.

Wait Not

I've had to teach myself all I'm slinging at you in these admonitions. I continue to apply effort of saying "no" to self, and can tell you this: *The sooner self-discipline is imposed, the broader base we build and the more quality life construction continues!* (This holds for most life situations.) If we wait until we're well into retirement to begin seriously looking at late life meaning and adaptation, it may well be too late, as the poem below illustrates:

Wait Not

Seize the moment swiftly passing
craft now for what's to be.
Linger not, as winds of change
affect the calmest sea.

With heart and mind make straight your course
a bearing clear to follow.
At destination, glad you'll be—
only folly waits the 'morrow.

Rouse! Awake—while it's called today!
New phase about to dawn!
For if you say, "O, another day. . ."
as the flower—'twill all be gone.

©2010 John Lewandoski

Belief: How We Each Perceive Aging

Each of us must set our own course for later years. Although your and my destinations—meaning life in the retirement phase and adapting to aging while there—are the same, each of us sees the outworking of our lives while there entirely differently. Within this valid individualism is where the proverbial soup gets thick, regarding how we understand the abstract aging process through which we must all travel.

Differing views come from differing belief origins. That's okay, too. Our *individual belief systems* have been shaped by circumstantial, moral, emotional, and spiritual factors developed through the living out and experience of life:

- our upbringing
- our circle of associates (family, work, social, friend influence)
- where we've been
- what we read
- who we listen to, and many more life elements too numerous to list here.

91

Our belief systems have literally formed who you and I *are* right now. Because each of us has an individual perception of abstract concepts or entities, such as time and aging, and because these values *are* abstract, none of us can make the ultimate determination of whether or not the concept of aging is considered good or bad for humanity.

Does it matter? What *does* matter is how each of us, in our own ways, as best possible, responds to aging by means of rationale assessment, resulting in gracious thought and activity that will impact ourselves and others favorably.

This means, primarily, we all need to determine:

- Is aging necessarily bad?
- What are our best ways of responding to aging?
- Are there professional means currently available to help us formulate and apply sound responses? (yes)

We need to draw sound, personal conclusions related to the aging process. If we do, and even if our conclusions differ somewhat, each of us will have a point-of-reference foundation upon which we can maintain life as prosperously as possible as aging increases.

This chapter will look at whether or not aging is necessarily an evil in our lives. The balance of the book deals with how to best respond to the aging/retirement linkage, and provides professional, formative approach in so doing.

Is Aging Necessarily Bad or Negative?

At first glance, it seems so. The medical and social sciences well outline the relentless effects of getting old.

MEDICAL SCIENCES:

First, for a very concise, actual, and 'fun-filled' unleashing of physical degeneration, do enjoy:

http://www.mayoclinic.com/health/aging (Reproduced verbatim, in completetion, below. Sorry…, all this is introduced for contrast and emphasis.)

"Aging: What to expect as you get older

Wonder what's considered a normal part of the aging process? Here's what to expect as you get older—and what to do about it.

By Mayo Clinic staff

Do you expect to find a few more wrinkles and gray hairs each time you look in the mirror? These are just some of the changes you're likely to notice as you get older. You're not necessarily at the mercy of Mother Nature, however. Here's a list of common aging-related changes—and what you can do to promote good health at any age.

Your Cardiovascular System

What's happening. *Over time, your heart muscle becomes less efficient—working harder to pump the same amount of blood through your body. In addition, your blood vessels lose some of their elasticity and hardened fatty deposits may form on the inner walls of your arteries (atherosclerosis). These changes make your arteries stiffer, causing your heart to work even harder to pump blood through them. This can lead to high blood pressure (hypertension) and other cardiovascular problems.*

What you can do about it. *To promote heart health, include physical activity in your daily routine. Try walking, swimming or other physical activities. Eat a healthy diet, including plenty of fruits, vegetables and whole grains. If you smoke, ask your doctor to help you quit. Your risk of heart disease will begin to fall almost immediately.*

Your Bones, Joints and Muscles

What's happening. *With age, bones tend to shrink in size and density—which weakens them and makes them more susceptible to fracture. You might even become a bit shorter. Muscles generally lose strength and flexibility, and you may become less coordinated or have trouble balancing.*

93

What you can do about it. Include plenty of calcium and vitamin D in your diet. Build bone density with weight-bearing activities, such as walking. Consider strength training at least twice a week, too. By stressing your bones, strength training increases bone density and reduces the risk of osteoporosis. Building muscle also protects your joints from injury and helps you maintain flexibility and balance.

Your Digestive System

What's happening. Constipation is more common in older adults. Many factors can contribute to constipation, including a low-fiber diet, not drinking enough fluids and lack of exercise. Various medications, including diuretics and iron supplements, may contribute to constipation. Certain medical conditions, including diabetes and irritable bowel syndrome, may increase the risk of constipation as well.

What you can do about it. To prevent constipation, drink water and other fluids and eat a healthy diet—including plenty of fruits, vegetables and whole grains. Include physical activity in your daily routine. Don't ignore the urge to have a bowel movement. If you're taking medications that may contribute to constipation, ask your doctor about alternatives.

Your Bladder and Urinary Tract

What's happening. Loss of bladder control (urinary incontinence) is common with aging. Health problems such as obesity, frequent constipation and chronic cough may contribute to incontinence—as can menopause, for women, and an enlarged prostate, for men.

What you can do about it. Urinate more often. If you're overweight, lose excess pounds. If you smoke, ask your doctor to help you quit. Pelvic muscle exercises (Kegel exercises) might help, too. Simply tighten your pelvic muscles as if you're stopping your stream of urine.

Aim for at least three sets of 10 repetitions a day. If these suggestions don't help, ask your doctor about other treatment options.

Your Memory

What's happening. *Memory tends to becomes less efficient with age, as the number of cells (neurons) in the brain decreases. It may take longer to learn new things or remember familiar words or names.*

What you can do about it. *To keep your memory sharp, include physical activity in your daily routine and eat a healthy diet. It's also helpful to stay mentally and socially active. If you're concerned about memory loss, consult your doctor."*

The effects of aging—probably the chief bane of humanity—are relentless.

Why We Age

There are several theories, some controversial. For example, much of the scientific community (especially neo-Darwinists—the evolution adherents), followed by much of medical and general analytical academia misses or, more likely, denies and ignores the fact that aging is rooted in moral/spiritual origins.

Many others, including myself, however, disagree: literally, we *age to death,* meaning the actual physiological and psychological deterioration of the human frame begins fading at birth. This viewpoint originates in the biblical account of man's fall from relationship with his Creator and is deeply theological in nature even though it's readily evident as soon as we are born aging begins.

Ooops…, I hear a *"What?!",* and see raised eyebrows. Wait; don't leave! It's all right on my end, my readers; I hope on yours as well. Let's talk about it….

Please know and realize I mean no criticism of any reader,

or theories held, whether religious or scientific. In fact, my own conclusion above isn't based on 'religion' at all, although many would so believe. My biblical credibility assessment of origins, resulting in aging, is based on rational analyzation, deduction, all through systematic, practical, unbiased study; i.e., my personal search for Truth. Notice I say "my" search. I don't mean to imply I have the only answer to origins, aging and death. If your understandings and conclusions differ, they are fully respected.

For purposes of this book, my intention here is to propose what not only I, but many far brighter and studied conclude to be an *extremely viable explanation for the aging phenomenon*. In other words, it's one of the theories. It is based on rational, not religious (although religion is involved), understanding of what the whole of scripture—the Old and New testaments—declares.

What is revealed, if read and understood objectively, is man's dilemma of aging originates when mankind, through free choice, decided to live above and contrary to the rules laid down by his Creator. The result is what I term a '3-D reality':

- disease
- decay/deterioration; i.e., *aging*
- death.

Of course, by extension, these thoughts take us into further realms of debating the validity of the Judeo-Christian Bible, itself, in terms of explaining the obvious plight of mankind. I won't diverge down that rabbit trail here.

Mankind certainly finds himself in a plight—an inescapable dilemma: we are born, age, die. Upon that fact, all of us can agree.

If we disagree on concepts of origins and man's continually degenerative dilemma—birth, aging, death—let's simply agree to disagree.

I really enjoy digging into the profound wonder of origin and destination, but will let it lie in slumber as further development within our context might prove counterproductive to our overall aim here—that being, *dealing* with aging. In a politically-fried age such as ours, most anything that touches 'religion' creates controversy.

To further discuss the possible validity of aging having a moral/spiritual base, do feel free to personally contact me via my website's email: www.personal-retirement-planning.com Peace.

Another View of the Aging Phenomenon

Among other theoretical slants of aging causality, here's one tied directly to gerontology. Dr. Mark Stibich, Ph.D., offers an overview from his published article:

Why We Age—Theories and Effects of Aging

The study of aging—gerontology—is a relatively new science that has made incredible progress over the last 30 years. In the past, scientists looked for a single theory that explained aging. There are two main groups of aging theories. The first group states that aging is natural and programmed into the body, while the second group of aging theories say that aging is a result of damage which is accumulated over time. In the end, aging is a complex interaction of genetics, chemistry, physiology and behavior.

Dr. Stibich is certainly correct in stating the complexity of aging.

Interestingly, however, genetics, chemistry, and physiology comprise their own broad category, *separate from* the last element he mentions—behavior. True enough, behavior can be affected by complex components and even aberrations, found among the first three, but none of the first three are at all influenced by the unmentioned moral factor, which is primarily integral to behavior. And by extension, the moral factor, alone, is certainly influenced by spiritual factors which, of course, takes us back to the possibility of the biblical explanation.

Stibich does state, though, that one of the two "… *main groups of aging theories…*" is that "…aging is natural and programmed into the body…"

The question then arises: what, how, or who originated that initial, programmed database!

Regardless of the ultimate origins of aging, the medical sciences are wondrous in presenting the understanding and technique we do have concerning ailment alleviation so integral to the aging dilemma.

Social sciences:

The social sciences also reveal much about aging's effects. Here, the effects are broader as they involve degeneration resulting from both physical and mental sources: depression, feeling cut-off from societal integration, boredom, feelings of worthlessness, dependence on others, suicide.

These sobering effects have a lot to do with the reason for, and the meaning of, Retirement's Missing Link, this book's title. Much of what is "missing", on the boomer's blind side, is that we need to prepare now to avert ill-effects, all we can, later. Certainly many of aging's effects are unavoidable, but much of its complications aren't if we do our homework.

WHAT YOU NEED TO KNOW:

- Reinforcement of our familiar mantra:
    - Don't wait until you reach old age to begin preparation for it!
- Although I've presented the Mayo Clinic 'golden years tour' through the ravages of aging, as grim as it is, throughout that entire report they continually illustrate that there are things that can be done to counter physical deterioration to some degree.
    - That's exactly my point as I endeavor to get readers to taking defensive action against aging in more philosophic and emotional ways.
        - The New Retirement paradigm offers a good step in that direction because its core emphasis is positive concerning retirement and aging among the boomer pre-retirement generation.

- The RSP (Retirement Success Profile) is the best 'launch pad' tool available to get you aimed in developing your own personal retirement/aging plan.
- Bottom line: if physical and mental retirement/aging degeneration isn't countered on a personal basis, niceties such as
  - depression,
  - feeling cut-off from societal integration
  - boredom
  - feelings of worthlessness
  - dependence on others
  - suicide

all have so much to offer!

Gerontological studies don't lie. Neither does real-life evidence....

Summary

The scientific community, and just plain common observation, tells us the social implications of getting old aren't exactly reason for jubilation.

So—is aging all bad?

It can be.

But...

11

Aging's Positives

ADDRESSED IN THIS CHAPTER:

• What "aging gracefully" really means.
• A few pluses only attainable in later years.

At the book's beginning we established that our time together in these pages was to be a journey. Journeys are characterized by not just happy times, but have a way of leading journeymen to encounter difficulty as well. Also, do you remember early-on the often used word *reality* or *realism?*

The previous chapter was a tough one. Although it initially revealed cause for some exhilaration and wonder in contemplating the Creation in which we find ourselves, it turned relatively gloomy, unsettling, and potentially upsetting. Dealing with the negative of late life aging and the immovable timeline along which it travels, is sobering at best. What's more, controversy surrounds how and why aging occurs in the first place.

Let's pick up the beat here by examining some genuinely *positive* features inherent in old age. (Are your eyebrows raised yet?) Yes, there *are* some; we'll take all we can get and maximize them to the hilt. Right? Though aging's positives don't entice us with urgency to experience them, later-life does possess some vital affirmatives not found in other life phases.

Graceful Aging

A good place to start is looking at what's called Graceful Aging. It's not really a true 'plus' of aging, but has value if applied in a mature way. Essentially, it's a catch-all term that performs more than one function. In a real sense, it *implies a denial* of aging's negatives by providing alternatives that hope to thwart such advances. Some common aging gracefully ideas center on:

- keeping face and hair youthful = aging gracefully
- trimming and toning the body = aging gracefully
- eating healthfully = aging gracefully
- staying active = aging gracefully
- maintain good social interaction = aging gracefully

Whenever someone is making an effort to either actually slow the aging process—or—is making themselves look as though they are: aging gracefully occurs.

Is this just staving off the inevitable? Maybe, but largely not. The key is to invest graceful effort in things of substance; beneficial areas of life that are helpful to the retiree's area of living involving self and others.

For example, the pursuit of Jack LaLanne-type health and fitness immortality is certainly wise and prudent. Pulling 70 boats with 70 people in them, for a mile and a half, in the water with hands tied, on your 70th birthday? No, but adapting Jack's lifelong commitment to eating quality food and getting plenty of exercise is hyper common sense. He's was the epitome of *physical* graceful aging.

Can this sort of longevity and power be attributed simply to the extraordinariness of the individual, such as LaLanne? Certainly genes play in, but his example of illustrating an unusual grace of living—well into his nineties—presents a strong model of what commitment to certain aspects of graceful aging can attain.

A good way baby boomers can get a grasp on their graceful aging 'IQ' is to ask some telling questions:

1. When you get together with friends do you compare

illnesses, aches, and pains, or partake in more beneficial, uplifting conversation?

2. When the topic of aging comes up in conversation, do
   you typically make it into a joke, like "Aging—isn't
   for sissies!"? Or, instead do you bemoan the trauma of
   getting older?

3. What about your life dreams? In discussion do you
   dwell on the past and what didn't work out, or talk
   about retirement plans you still hold dear?

4. When you're with your grown children, do you tell
   them stories about your past or find ways to offer sound
   advice toward their life success?

5. Do you think more about aging or what's yet ahead in
   your retirement plans?

6. Are you more into anti-aging products or willing to
   accept the grey and wrinkles?

7. Is your retirement life glass half empty or half full?

Think seriously on these situations. Your aging gracefully
barometer can tell you whether you dwell in the present and
look to the future within your retirement planning, or if a
preoccupation with the past and current negative is more your
prevailing attitude. These are serious life issues. Attitude shifts
or changes could be in store.

Graceful aging *is* more than a cover phrase to make getting old look good; it has merit. Boomers do well to consider
the ways of those already-arrived retirees applying substantive
principles of aging gracefully, noting the difference between
their lives of relative meaning, generally superior overall de-
meanor, even fulfillment—as opposed to—the lives of those
who just schlep along in a continual state of late-life mediocrity, or worse.

If we apply mindsets of honest positives as we age, seriously
and with diligence, we can realize life value in a way that does
grace us *and* those we touch. What can be of more value!

Retirement: A gateway to clear thought

Another authentic positive of the retirement segment of aging is having far more time-to-think potential than we'd had earlier.

Your first impression of this idea may conjure visions of front porch rocking chairs or similar. That could be the setting, but isn't the real gist here. Once retirement becomes real, in most instances it's amazing how quiet life can be—if that's wanted. Often it is wanted, and almost always is a Martha Stewart "good thing" that should be secured.

Retire and breathe a bit—or a season. Let thoughts reside between the ears for more than a millisecond's duration—usual fare during the mid-life stage. Retirement is, after all, about leisure held in good balance with other aspects of retirement living.

With the fray of life's pandemonium behind us, a far greater opportunity to mentally explore pursuits, which earlier just weren't prime life focal points, or even opportunities for that matter, is now availed.

As comparative illustration:

Consider life during the *career environment*—trying to think and concentrate on something other than the mundane was difficult. Squallin' kids, traffic, barking dogs, unending phone calls, demanding bosses, noisy neighbors, not enough sleep all kept us at bay from pursuing deeper thinking, passions, goals, or curiosities that could have been fulfilling.

Now consider the *retirement environment*—sitting lakeside in Maine. Or in a comfy chair in your apartment living room! Or on a porch rocking chair. I mean, you can almost 'hear' yourself think! What's more, note the almost melodic tone to "retirement environment". It even sounds good!

Is having time to sort out life and think through things that once offered little more than sound byte duration, a part of aging? You bet. You only get this perk as you age and the din around you subsides.

In our retirement we can find ourselves in a mind-expansion arena, so to speak. We are able to reformulate and navigate thinking in ways the fray of life didn't formerly allow.

From that reformulation, productive avenues can develop that lead to perceiving life on a grander scale.

All this is positive and usually isn't customary during pre-retirement because of life's complexity of demands. It's certainly an indirect positive of aging.

Letting Time Sliiiiide . . .

Let's revisit life at Pennswood Village for a moment (Sundays at my mother's place, Chapter 1).

I'll never forget the lifestyle impression Ma and her elder friends at the Village made upon me. They had a gross advantage I, at the time, could only imagine. My life then was measured by standards of an energized bunny; their lives were so much more gracefully measured: No–big-hurry! My life was squeezed by daily pursuits of raising a family and making a living; theirs fully lacked that time-related stress. The attitude was that tomorrow was another day and would take care of mending in what might have been missed today. As the welcome sign entering Maine reads, "The way life should be."

Many a Sunday by late afternoon, amid their company, I'd be mentally planning out the next day's/week's work and duties, thinking about getting home to take care of detail there before getting to bed, with it all done, so I could set the alarm and be up and at 'em come daybreak.

One could say gracefully measured time equates to being able to say—"No—big—*deal!*"

(Interestingly, attempting to slow aging—in our sixties, seventies, eighties—is the exact inverse of impetuous youth who try to speed up the movement of time and its effects! What a classic example of the riddle that is life.)

More Good Things

The positive elements of late life need our consideration even before we arrive. Understanding the subtleties elemental freedoms of aging delivers helps bring about that pre-retirement settledness I mentioned earlier on. Fear of the unknown is lessened; confidence in approaching getting older is increased.

To illustrate the beauty of genuine aging subtleties, consider with aging comes a keener appreciation of

- contemplation
- quietness
- thoughtfulness.

As the relative commotion of preceding decades recedes, exposing the mind to far less clutter, *a freedom* to think deeply and with clarity *arises:* the experience can be like a light bulb being turned on in a dark room! Such ability can cause earlier nagging thought issues to surface and be, potentially, finally resolved. In earlier life, they may have been suppressed, yielding to more crucial issues at the time. It is when we have **time** to really work through what were once thought entanglements, that processing, sorting out, and resolution can more easily occur.

(I realize some of my pre-retirement readers may have difficulty relating to this slowdown; you're still in high gear mode. Believe me, however, pensiveness does appear—graciously. I speak for many I know, in their sixties mainly, who indicate this same mental transition from hectic thought to ones more of subdued, contemplative nature. This isn't to say living is shutting down—not at all—but rather that *approaches* to living aren't as frenetic as in earlier times; frankly, what a relief!)

Later in life, real friends will have been established, and those that remain, well valued! The peripheral social dealings of earlier times are then found to be relatively trivial, allowing valuable depth of enjoyment with those most dear; deep, kindred spirit. I've seen some of the closest and endearing of relationships solidified in later life.

Accumulated wisdom and experience will yield an increasing self-confidence, which can translate into applied wisdom; i.e., conveying to others, in humility, the wealth of what only years of living can have instilled in your unique personhood.

The Cynic

Are there positives that arise as we age? Yes, there are. I suppose the cynic can relegate them to sour grapes rationalization; i.e., *looking* for something we can call positive when, in actuality, there's little or none to be found.

Although that assessment can be true, it's wholly, subjectively, negative. Being of positive persuasion isn't sour grapes reality. It's accurately seizing what is good and right, and then maximizing it to the hilt in our life experience. Again, a cynic or skeptic might imply all this is merely mind games and self-deception; i.e., aging stinks, and that's that.

Al contraire, I say, as an old country gospel song by June Carter-Cash encourages:

Keep on the sunny side, always on the sunny side
Keep on the sunny side of life.
It will help us every day, it will brighten all the way
If we keep on the sunny side of life.

Simple admonition? You bet.

Easy to do? No. That's why she wrote the song. That's why the cynic *needs* the song, even though its message is believed to be relative nonsense.

Is conjuring up positives little more than playing mind games with a relentless, aging foe? You decide....

Is aging at all easy...?

It's a matter of heart-realization-reality: as the heart thinks, the mind can so administer.

There are fine lines here. It's up to you, me—and the cynic—to view aging from our respective vantage points. From there each of us must decide, in relation to it, how we shall then live.

WHAT YOU NEED TO KNOW:

- Perception of aging positives originates in a heart and mind usually favorable toward life in general. The inverse, unfortunately, is also true.

- Later-life affords time for contemplation and wonder. Such times can draw the mind into a sense of being, a presence of mind not hindered by all the trappings of worldly life, once so common.

- Contemplation and taking time for deeper thinking can often lead to a clear awareness of solving earlier, nagging thought issues that never had been resolved.

12

Crossroads, Decisions, Building Roadblocks

ADDRESSED IN THIS CHAPTER:

• Right and wrong decision making: The battlefield is the mind.
• Yesterday is a good place to visit, but not to live.
• Aging's deceptions are nasty!

In the last chapter we concluded though the outward frame—our bodies—indeed decline in strength and vigor as the years progress, the inward man can actually be renewed in later years because of accumulated wisdom, experience, and actual post-career time available to put all that to use.

Also in Chapter 11, a few pluses of later life were enumerated; more could have been. My intention was not to scavenge for an impressive list of goodies in attempt to make warm 'n' fuzzy that which really isn't. Plainly, life positives diminish in number as the years mount even though, thankfully, much positive good can be experienced. And the good is often the result of good decision making.

Life Crossroads

Although life decision points are more prevalent in pre-retirement life, many also exist all through retirement and into old age. It's up to each of us to make wise choices at the crossroads where difficult life issues demand going one direction or another.

How these crossroads are handled during retirement is pivotal because they contribute greatly to whether life will be satisfying or not. If, especially prior to retirement, we've learned to *pattern our thinking to positive choice advantage,* it will spill over considerably into later retirement and old age—a time when balanced, life reality choices are *crucial* to overall good and well-being, to ourselves and those we touch.

To get our minds trained to produce any sort of good, against a backdrop of physiological aging, is no small task. Nor is it anything impossible to do! It's a matter of

- squarely approaching difficult life reality issues
- determining wise choices through acquisition of truthful reality
- exercising good resolve, then following through.

Every good thing produced in life begins with a determination to reject that which, in our inner being, we know combats positive outcomes. In short, *we must erect mental roadblocks* against ideas we know aren't productive, even though they entice through ease or attractiveness in the short term.

The key to patterning right thinking must be found in our own initiative. Frankly, for some it's relatively easy, seemingly having an innate desire to make orderly that which isn't; others just wing it—the "what will be will be", "come what may" sort of thing.

Your reading of this sort of book probably means winging it, in your estimation, is folly. Agreed! If it's important enough to affect our lives, isn't it important enough to cause a mustering up of incentive, even if so doing doesn't necessarily come naturally?

More people fail for lack of aim or purpose than for most any other reason. If you are fortunate enough to have initiative, half the battle's won. If you don't, pray for, meditate toward, contemplate about—do *something* to attain it. Life, in general, is an overall battle of good versus evil, positive opposing negative, on many, many levels.

The Battlefield is the Mind

There are battlefields where guns and tanks rage; there is also the battlefield within—the mind. That's where our choices, decisions, and follow-through actions are made.

Regardless of type of outside influence—positive, negative, or indifferent—we process all experiential activity, thought, and circumstance within the context of mind *decision making*.

What determines the *direction* of the decision making? Several things: point of reference, conscience (determined by our values), personal inclination, ambition, quality of information, and much more. (Topics for another day…)

During retirement and getting older, the decisions of how we choose to perceive life difficulties can be the determinants of battles we win or lose in the warfare against aging.

The mind, where we ultimately determine our perspectives and actions, must adopt a **'put on /lace up marching boots'** attitude. The battle, into which we enter as aging increases, is *the battle for establishment of quality life perspectives* amid the ever-present, progressive deterioration of our outer frame.

This cries aloud for development of a sound steeling of ourselves where wishy-washiness can be all too common. In other words as we age, and the frequency of aging positives diminishes, we need to have been rooted in what we know we've decided *beforehand* to be right; sound decisions on generally tough reality, made ahead of time—now—during pre-retirement.

Thank you for bearing with me with this do-it-now repetition on my behalf. As with a good advertisement, it's the 'repetition of the ad' that often is more important than actual content in producing results. I keep repeating the *prepare now* concept because getting a knowledgeable understanding, early, leading to good decision making—*while we aren't under pressure to have to make them, as we may well be later*—is prudent. It's crucial.

I talk to too many older retirees who now struggle with unproductive, retirement/aging life patterns. In most cases it's too late to change ingrained thinking patterns that lead nowhere. To large extent this relates back to poor preparation—a lack of seriously thinking ahead when these folks were in pre-retirement.

Part of aging gracefully, previously discussed, means to put into effect revitalized and *well-rooted thoughts and emotions,* despite the aging process. This is vital because on the back of aging ride seeds of opposition to all that's *good,* ready to sow discord in and through our entire thought and emotional makeup. It's at those difficult crossroads of life reality we need to choose to not let negative seeds of opposition take root. It's at those crossroads, that if we've *already* come to terms with many of later life's difficult issues, aging gracefully will be as natural as saying "hello."

Note: I write in the above paragraph, *"...well-rooted thoughts and emotions..."* Remember, back in Chapter 6, I cautioned against the potential deception of reliance on emotions and feelings not rooted in what we've come to determine as truth and reliability? Thought perspective and emotion are valid if we're reasonably certain of a credible information base.

Do become informed about later-life ideas and likely eventualities. Attempt to sort between retirement ballyhoo and substantive senior matter that counts. Learn to walk circumspectly. Then let the mind constructfully build on a sure foundation of later-life material that, even pre-retirement, applies to you personally.

I wish I could write to you, each reader, within the context of your personal world, concerning the crossroads of life you are experiencing, or likely will be as retirement nears. Obviously, that's impossible in a public book format, but keep in mind it's very possible via the RSP (Retirement Success Profile). It's that very tool that enables you and me to connect on your personal retirement issues and decisions—the tough stuff of personal retirement planning.

The Ghost of Retirement—Yet to Come

Before we get to any crossroads of difficult issues, let's add a little serious fantasy to our discussion.

Suppose—just suppose—right now you could be figuratively catapulted forward and observe how your life would be playing out—how you'd actually live and feel—say, maybe five years into your retirement. What do you think you'd see? Would you be doing well? Poorly? Would you be glad you had made the decision to retire when you did? Would you have planned for retirement differently? Regardless of what you'd find, chances are some changes would be made.

What a life bonus such fantasy foresight could be! If you could see what life would be like before having lived it, based on what you saw, you'd have a chance to make changes before heading back to the present.

Although reality can't provide any such crystal ball, certainly, what we're about here, can provide an informative, tempered with common sense, look ahead.

Do you remember 'Mr. Miserable': Ebenezer Scrooge, the principle character in Charles Dickens' 1843 novel, *A Christmas Carol?* It was the Ghost of Christmas Yet to Come who transported old Scrooge to just such a crystal-ball vantage point. Did it ever open *his* eyes! He was given opportunity to make grandiose changes in life perspective—which he did. Instantly!

I'm not saying that I've been transported by any ghost, or that either you or I are to be lumped in with miserly, miserable Scrooge. The point this wonderfully impactful fantasy so well illustrates is *the great advantage of being able to make some determination for the future, because we **can** gain at least some insight to it—today!*

There's nothing fantastic or magical about this sort of thing. All that's needed is pursuit of knowledge (especially about yourself!), rooted in truth, then acted upon.

Of course, at this point in time, I have no need to be wisked ahead to see my retirement because I'm already here. But I wasn't always. And I'm not that far into it even now—this could go on for another twenty years or so.

Considering myself fortunate, the years of interest and inquiry into retirement and gerontology I enjoyed prior to my retirement are, in a way, analogous to the fantasy journey of transport that changed thought and perspective for old Scrooge. Because of that learning season (yet on-going, of course), I've been transported ahead, as it were, to view a later life panorama *far broader than what contemporary society and culture could ever have delivered.* In a way, I've had the opportunity to 'be there' before I actually arrived. You can, too—by taking all this *seriously* now.

Recently, upon beginning to assemble this writing, I found the opportunity to sit me down a bit and reflect on where I'd be today *if,* today, all my eggs were in the usual retirement basket of money, leisure, keeping busy, and dodging the bullets of advancing age—the very things of which our general fall/ winter phase of life is usually thought to be composed.

Were it not for the blessing of being motivated to have learned more of retirement and gerontology, *I likely would be a retiree who*

- keeps 'busy' (busyness gets old and helps you become old)
- would be somewhat plagued by the loss of the advantages the career years had provided (might even wish I hadn't retired)
- might still wonder 'who I really am' (this will be developed in later chapters)
- would still be wondering what fulfillment in life really means
- couldn't adapt well to profound life perspective changes and decisions that retirement most definitely delivers
- dodges the serious need of caring for physical and mental health
- still wishes I could develop sensible and committed attitude toward later life's most difficult issues, which yet lie ahead
- would lack the "settledness" of which I often speak
- would see ever-encroaching age as an absolute spoiler of life.

113

Like old Scrooge and me, you are in the same fortunate position to avert going into retirement without the rest of the story. Based on Scrooge's journey forward, his personal life perspective was greatly broadened, adjusted, and made happier. In kind, once you more internalize retirement and aging are far deeper than what societal culture promotes, your perspectives will adjust to your gain; you'll be building a broad-based, truly firm foundation for the biggest transition of your life.

Life Crossroads Requiring Decision and Courage

John Lennon didn't live long enough to experience the reality of 'yesterday' in light of his brief today. He wrote, *"Yesterday. All my troubles seemed so far away. Now it looks as though they're here to stay. Oh, I believe in yesterday."*

We can choose to live among memories that bring some solace to troubled, current reality. But I've heard it said, more wisely than John Lennon perceived:

"Yesterday is a good place to visit, but not to live."

There's good reason for this notion: it's easy to lament and feel sorry for ourselves. If our thought life continually dwells in memories of yesterday, lamenting our displeasure with today, living of today will be crowded out, which limits the making of *future* memories.

If we are so busy visiting the past, we have no time to live today.

Certainly poor health and situational issues of our today can make the most positive among us yearn for what has been a time when life was simply better; more agreeable. Regardless of conditions that may develop with time, however, we nevertheless are called to live within them, difficult though it can be.

Memories, as compared to living life in the now, are fantasy. This is not to at all imply insensitivity to cherished thoughts embedded in our souls, for they add much wealth to balanced thinking. The issues arise when memories *govern* and, worse, limit a sense of vibrancy of life today, rendering daily, current life of lesser value than it could and should be. This can be depressively dangerous.

Today is tomorrow's yesterday. If we don't make something of today, come tomorrow, today will be another bad memory! If this cycle continually repeats, bad memories continue to mount, forcing us to live even further back in time, in that 'place' where only a pleasing memory can be found for relief.

When we're down, yesterday can be a good place to visit, but not to check-in; the rates are too high!

Today is free! In fact, it's a *gift*. Maybe you've heard it said, *"Today is a gift. That's why it's called—the present."* Trite, maybe, but on the money.

Mind Focus Counters Aging's Deceptions

If we are to vitally live in the present as we age, how will that be achieved as infirmities—physical, mostly—creep into daily circumstances? Good *decisional warfare* needs to be imposed.

Decisional warfare? It's my own term describing the necessity of realizing that during the increased aging experience, we are in battle to maintain quality life. Learning to make as *clear decisions* as possible to take the bad stuff captive, while promoting the good, is a wise step in quality, long-life maintenance.

Aging *Deception*: I Can't Do Things Anymore

With increasing physical infirmities comes the tendency to concentrate on the limitations they cause. How much better to *decide* transference of such wasted negative energy, from what can't be corrected, to areas of positive application!

I don't mean to imply this shift of mental focus is an easy, sloping slide, lined on both sides with blooming, fragrant, roses—no, no, no. When we ache, we *ache*. Life has a lot of ache. Learning to get positive, when our nature would tell us to gripe and complain, is downright difficult—something like ascending an uphill grade with shifting sand under our feet.

Combat boots, comrades! Either we are aggressive in this battle of the mind, or we let the *thief of deception* come to plunder, steal, and destroy.

As a personal example, although at sixty-five I'm not yet 'old', I've struggled with an ongoing health issue that has seemed endless. I still struggle; now, as I write. During the worst of episodes, it's been a continual battle to *decide* to get out of a hurting/negative thought pattern and into one that's relatively beneficial. I'm admittedly not an over-achiever in this capacity but, in fact, have learned the true advantage of steering my thinking priorities toward what is good and re-deeming, amid the fray.

Some think this is playing mind games. No, it's more about taking command of decision making, applying resolve, and fueling it all with *knowing* it's the right and best thing to do. What does doing the *right* thing have to do with it? To answer that takes us in a whole new direction; one definitely worthy of the time, but not in our retirement/aging connection here.

It works; that's the point. If we don't take command of our thinking, by rooting it in worthwhile aim and thought, we *further* fall victim to the deception that suggests worthless-ness, resignation, and defeat. Nothing good can come from such situation.

So—obviously not having yet arrived in 'old age', we start now to begin training ourselves to *side with* ourselves *against* the enemy: deception.

Later life physical limitations and difficulties are certain. We need to be *deciding* that griping and sorry-feeling will only worsen as time goes on, if we so allow.

Now is the time to decide, putting into practice if we haven't, aligning with that "sunny side of life" mentality, nurturing it along, more and more, as we grow in age and wisdom.

How might this positive shift be ultimately expressed? This transfer of mind focus—from what degrades and destroys, to what builds up and creates—may be guided toward personal or interpersonal activity and expression, maybe both. We may help ourselves by creating new paths of thought and expression, or determining we have capability, through accumulated life experiences, to considerably help others. Again, maybe both. The idea is to not be led into what can be aging's darkness when so much life can be had in the light.

In other words, during our career years some passions and desires likely have been laying in dormancy during the recent decades of heavy career concentration and family responsibilities. Probably we haven't given serious thought to *how we'll need to think and perceive life* once retirement and increased aging arrive.

All through those years, experience and learning, right up to and including now, has been accumulating. The trick, therefore, is to now (if we haven't already) *begin to at least see the need* to convert that wealth of accumulation to long-term good use, for our own benefit and that of others.

Aging will inevitably take some toll on our ability to remain physically and mentally vital. The good news, however, is that its most destructive tendencies are on a tether of sorts; it cannot control our thinking. Remember, *we are what we think,* and the battleground of thought is certainly our mind. Win *there,* and we maintain the ultimate upper hand in living, come what may.

You may notice I haven't created a how-to list of specifics of "what to do in retirement". Instead, my intent is to *stir awareness* that we need to be aligning our thinking along the lines of broad action concepts that can be applied later.

Aging *Deception*: I See Myself as Old— All I've Done is Now Lost

This is one of the most destructive, slippery traps of aging there is. Although aging presents many liabilities, we have in us what it takes to strongly counter its many threats against our overall welfare:

Yes, the outward frame is perishing, but unless dementia or related mental ills are involved, the inner person is not.

This truth must be internalized in our heart of hearts: You are still *'you'*. The real "you" (in later life) is a stronger, broader compilation of your personal essence: time yields experience, which yields understanding, comprehension and hopefully wisdom—all being outright foreign, by comparative degree, in our youth.

We can't avert aging, but we can counter it by remembering that at this later date in life we now have potential value never before possible. Launching from that solid pier, so to speak, we can therefore make definitive decisions to thumb the nose at aging and purpose to set sail in a new sea—utilizing the cargo of wisdom and experience we've been accumulating all along.

As with much in this book, I speak here from personal experience. In the years before taking official retirement, as I'd work at gaining solid perspective of those years to come, it became increasingly obvious there would come the time I'd have to transfer physical life activity—the me who could always 'do'—to the *me* I really am, regardless of physical condition.

This very concept of finding out *who we are at core,* and what to do with it later on, is part of the centrality of this book. We haven't gotten there yet, but you'll relate to what I say here before long.

PERSONAL STATEMENT:

- the writing of this very book
- having a personal retirement consulting business
- embarking on the established activity of publishing—

these are exact examples of *not* seeing myself as old and worthless!

Of course, the time may come when I cease to write and offer counsel. When the time arrives to lay down the pen, and likely even the interpersonal dialogs and all—

I hope to be able to have no regrets that purposeful carrying on, past mid-life career, was precisely the right thing to do.

Whatever "carrying on" means to you, do so. Go for it; see with new eyes and extended vision. Be encouraged!

Building Our Own Defensive Roadblocks

Usually when we think 'roadblocks', we think them to be impediments to where we're headed, figuratively or in daily life reality—as in being on the Schuylkill Expressway (main artery to Philadelphia) during rush hour: *roadblock*, not traffic jam!

We can, however, erect our own roadblocks, to our advantage, as an offensive against Old Man Time.

Let me illustrate, from a 'happy place'. This event takes us to the rocky coast of Maine—where the mountains meet the sea....

My wife, Audrey, and I have a love of classic New England, strongly including Maine's coastline area. I can remember one warm fall day a couple years ago, snooping around the coast with dreams in our heads of buying some sort of abode, and then take in the fresh coastal air for a late-life season—someday, maybe.

We followed our noses wherever they led, happening upon a small, quaint older home somewhere around Damariscotta: old siding, weathered cedar shingles, window frames that looked as if they'd withstood many a Nor'easter; even the remains of an old skiff laying against a paint-less picket fence.

The place was the real thing. It had long lived the rigors of coastal Maine, not unlike us retirees having done the same with the challenges of life!

The doors and windows were open, a panel truck in the yard, and a man was hard at work slowing the disrepair the years had wreaked—shoring up what the years had not yet taken.

We stopped and chatted a bit. He indicated he'd made a decision to buy the older 'autumn season' cottage in effort to preserve what life yet remained in it.

The gentleman was exercising an ability he possessed: *taking action* in positively slowing down what time and nature, otherwise, were intent on slowly decaying. Sound familiar?

The fact is—the old cottage had value; in fact, *more* value because of its age.

Taking charge of our futures, to the degree we are humanly capable, will contribute greatly in withstanding our own Nor'easters….

That treasure near the sea, today, years later? My hunch is, were we to return to that sweet cottage location, we'd find it weathering, 'aging gracefully', in a clime so characteristic of the craggy, picturesque coastline that kisses the sea.

Aging, like the weather, brings indisputable difficulties that deteriorate what we've known to be whole and vibrant. The resolute Mainer interrupted, and to a point, *road-blocked a cycle of deterioration*. We can do likewise. Especially the emotional effects of aging can be slowed or even interrupted for a time—realistically, not with pills or some new snake oil, but through thinking that originates somewhere in learning the general principle of overcoming evil with good.

Granted, I'm painting with a broad paintbrush using that worn, yet valid "positive thinking" concept. Positive thinking is advantageous in helping us rise above that which is wrong, negative, despised, or all three. And to be positive, as opposed to negative, usually leads to light and not darkness; overcoming general 'evil' with good.

Is positive thinking, therefore, the panacea that transports us through the difficulties of getting old? Not really. Many make a name for themselves (and usually plenty of money) capitalizing on distorted positivism, as if "thinking positively" is an end in itself, leading to conquering all our ills. It goes deeper than that.

I realize all this I'm offering here centered in "good" and "positivism" may be little more, to some, than a rosy-scented approach to fixing a poison ivy problem.

It's true: we can't 'think' our way, positively, through what appears to be nothing but the negative reality of physical, and too often mental, deterioration connected to increased aging.

Positive thinking *is* nonsense *if not rooted in firm foundation that provides realistic alternative* to ascend above the waning of the physical frame. We can 'work-up' positive attitudes, which can endure briefly, but they crumble if they are based on little more than wishful thinking and not what we sense to be realism and truth.

So, *where's* the realism already?!

What I'm saying is that each of us must find, within our individual understanding of how life works, some degree of realistic, firm foundation; meaning sound and reasonable beliefs. This core stuff of life—of our being actually—obviously leads us toward spiritual elements which transcend the physical. Here we enter the life-*meaning* dynamic, as well as all thought that gets us past the five senses and physical world around us.

In Part II I'll elaborate much more fully on our spiritual connection to real life. Suffice to say here—*everyone* possesses a connection to spirituality because being spiritual, broadly defined, comprises thinking on that which is immaterial and non-corporeal. You can be an atheist, never grace the entrance to a church building, and be very spiritual.

So, what's a good roadblock to erect against the advance of aging? Answer: coming to actual awareness and settled determination in our minds where we stand in our relation to the meaning of birth, life, death, and the hereafter.

I certainly cannot do this for you, nor vice-versa. I can show you where to look; but you'll have to find your own path to Truth. Nor can either of us have the best of the two worlds of indecision; *that 'place' where so many pre-retirees live;* that "what will be will be" indifference; that not really seeking out what we can come to determine as bedrock foundation for our very existence.

Where's realism? It's where you, and what you find to be Truth, meet.

As you can see, retirement, aging, destiny *is* complex. It's oh, so easy, to jettison all this complexity and just concentrate on looking to enjoying retirement! Friend, I *do* hear ya…, especially if times are early, and you are just *thinking* about retirement a little at this point in time. If you are a young pre-retiree, you may find these confrontations to aging very distant.

They are only *relatively* distant.

Remember old Scrooge? His wake-up call, not too late in life, eventually helped not only his personal existence, but maybe even more so, that of Bob Cratchit and others. *Now's* the time—to at least begin filling in the gaps society isn't telling you about your personal future—that "missing link". It's just down the road a piece.... You can find it, if you'll seek for it with all your heart.

I realize I'm like a State Trooper—in-your-face, delivering a warning instead of a ticket. I mean no offense. This "warning" is a heads-up, only designed to humbly offer an awareness that excessive speeding can really kill, and stimulates (or should) our sensitivities that we aren't the only ones on the road.

WHAT YOU NEED TO KNOW

- The war against aging means we wear combat boots in our thinking! It's the battle for establishment of quality life perspectives *amid* the negative of physiological deterioration.

- As we age, a vigilant mind focus, on a daily basis, is what counters the two biggest, hardcore deceptions aging relentlessly throws at us:

  1. "I can't do things anymore!"

  2. "I see myself as old—all I've done is now lost!"

- Although space in this book won't permit expansion of these two prime retirement/aging maladies, suffice to say here it's crucially important to recognize these aging 'demons' for who they are.

- Part II, ideally coupled with the RSP (Retirement Success Profile), helps you form a firm foundation which counters negative self-perception.

13

Good Decisions

ADDRESSED IN THIS CHAPTER:

• Elemental right/wrong techniques in solid decision making
• A retirement example: analytical versus intuitive decision making

This chapter carries a lot of importance. As you are now aware, we've covered a lot of territory already that points to a crucial action all of us must take, constantly—making good decisions!

Nothing new about this, right? Think about it for a moment: most everything we do on a daily basis involves decision making. We open our eyes to the morning and immediately have to decide whether to get up or slumber a tad more. And so it goes throughout the day....

If you've read this far, you know planning for retirement and the last roughly third of life involves some major decision making. Or at least it should.

Remember much of the book mantra so far?

• Get the facts (truth, not hearsay or loose opinion)
• Don't let emotion rule
• Make sound judgment calls

What's another description of making sound judgment calls? Answer: making sound *decisions*.

The further I've gotten in writing this book, the more I've been reminded decision making, itself, can be problematic.

Some people find it easy to qualify elements of decision making and have little trouble in working quality outcomes as result. Others get overwrought or uneasy with decision making, usually winding up making bad decisions or, sometimes, none at all.

What makes the difference between such individuals? Well, that answer isn't simple. Why? Because we're all so different in terms of:

- genes (predisposition; how we're made—all out of our control)
- knowledge, or lack of it (good or bad; correct or flawed)
- experiences (beneficial or jaded)
- values, morality, spiritual sensitivity
- attitude (shaped by all the above)
- emotion (that fickle component than can mess with everything!)

As with many repetitive actions in life, including making up our minds, the more we perform a given action, the more ingrained it becomes in our life patterning. There's a double-edged sword in all this, however, common to us all—be careful: *quality in, quality out; junk in, junk out.*

How many of us really understand there are some elemental right/wrong techniques in solid decision making? Many people think decision making happens automatically. That can be the case; most always it's not.

During most of my earlier life, I reacted to decision making based on emotion or being too swift to act. In addition, prevailing circumstances coupled with wrong attitudinal perspective contributed to poor decision patterning. Messy, huh? Have you ever been there, too?

This combination of school-of-hard-knocks, experience and, thankfully, study over the years have combined in offering what seems to be a generally good approach to making decisions that offer good and beneficial outcomes concerning most any given decisional topic at hand. I'll share them with you below.

Of course, our main goal is to apply all this decision making to retirement and aging, but I think you'll also find these broad decision making concepts beneficial amid the ka-zillion choices, big and small, that must be made in a lifetime.

Dealing With Decisions

Scatter-brained, ditsy, wishy-washy, double-minded—and many other such terms describe shallow root in the human thinking processes. Bad decisions all too often result when haphazard thinking processes replace more systematic technique.

Have you ever met someone who appears to be all over the place concerning making up their mind? *They can't seem to differentiate between a main, important topic and related sub-topics that are comparatively unimportant.* This all too often results in poor decisions or none at all.

GETTING THINKING IN RIGHT ORDER:

1. *Get to the core issue amid the clutter*

Let's say you're 60 and are thinking of retirement at age 62. You have conflicting thoughts, questions and outcomes swirling concerning when the best time for you to pull the prime career plug may be. <u>You have to cognitively determine</u> what's *core and central*, in terms of importance—to retiring at 62 or—*not* to retire at 62. A simple yes or no is to be the ultimate tie-breaker. Sounds simple, right?

For example, some of the swirling scenarios and thoughts may include:

- you're tired of career and want a clean break
- your wife would like you to be home with her
- your daughter's family would like you to relocate closer to theirs
  but
- staying on the job will continue to fatten the nest-egg
- you're going to miss career friends and lifestyle if you pull out
- you may not know what to do with your time after a while

and

• your health is only so-so, and you've been medically advised to jump the career ship while life can still be enjoyed.

Note the first three bullets are reasons to retire; the next three reasons not to do so. And then there's the last reason...

The point here is that seven solid—all valid—reasons exist whether or not to take retirement at 62. If the list continues to swirl in your thinking, *without determining what's the most important,* no choice at all is likely to come forth. All the points have merit, but the seventh issue—health matters—may be the most important. (I've segregated the health issue, for point of illustration, to make it appear the most important.)

Let's, however, look at the entire picture. Although rational health reasoning may at first seem to be the most important determination suggesting you retire at 62, note how easy dwelling on the other six peripheral issues can be. Sure—everybody knows "the most important thing is your health", but oh, so easy it is to allow the other six pro and con reasons to take emotional precedence, causing constant wondering, back and forth, that some of the other issues are really as important. (And in fact, all things considered, that may just *be* the case!)

The bottom line is this: amid the entire emotional versus rational fray of conflicting ideas, when push comes to shove, a yes or no answer, to what deep down you know to be the *core* issue, is crucially necessary.

That **most important** *of all the ideas must be determined and segregated from the rest, for until it is, no concrete decisional game plan can be drawn.*

Truth to tell, sifting through all the detail of multiple and conflicting ideas is downright hard work, especially on major life issues. It's easier to keep the ideas flying around in our thinking than to have to make a commitment to that one point we know in our heart of hearts is *the* most important single decision factor requiring a determination of

yes, DO it—or—no, DON'T do it*!*

2. If the enormity of that most important decision is too great; break it down into smaller chunks

Sometimes a decision is so enormous, we can't get our minds around the whole thing.

Using our same example of retiring or not at 62, when you consider the entirety of the issue your mind is flooded with all the component parts:

- If I retire at 62, should we sell the house and downsize?
- If we sell, should we move to a new, cheaper area?
- Moving will mean changing churches, leaving old friends, starting over.
- Will quality health care facilities be available where we'd like to move; especially important as we continue to age?

It's impossible to answer all these questions, and more, at one time. The key is to *pursue realistic, factual answers, one question at a time; then go on to the next one.* It's the step by step process that relieves the exasperation of trying to tackle the entire decision as a whole.

*3. Make a decision based on **who** you actually **are**, not as a reason to scratch some emotional itch*

Continuing our example, let's assume you finally have decided to retire at 62. Good for you! You've broken down the big decision and pursued answers to each of the smaller decision chunks:

- First, maybe you looked into geographic areas that have always been attractive and are in your current price range.
- Next, you looked into health care facilities and churches in the region, and made a good determination you'd fit into the social climate of the area.
- So, far so good! Bit by bit, you've chewed away at the smaller, multiple details of the larger decision and, voila—the making of the big decision has, more or less, been worked out by first answering the smaller components. So, all in all, you've analytically decided retiring at 62 holds together. The whole, indeed, is the sum of its parts.

But—now enters a further personal aspect to it all: whether

to go the 55-and-over route, *or* to buy that smaller home on a lake with fireplace and lots of wood on the land to feed it.

What have now entered the decision making equation are the personal factors of likes and dislikes, which often rival strengths and weaknesses. Care is needed in this sort of decision making because it's easy to make a decision based on what emotions suggest *'will make you happier'* (scratching some emotional itch), rather than on what true intuition and common sense otherwise suggest as solid reality.

We're dealing with a balance issue here. Unless we can tame emotional suggestion with common sense, we easily head for a bad decision.

This isn't to say what we feel (emotion) isn't important; it is.

The trouble brews when runaway emotion overtakes our real nature and sensibilities. We need to not miss who we actually are when our heads are screwed on properly, and *what we're capable of handling,* realistically. Emotion sometimes causes us to see through rose-colored glasses, as it were...

4. Seeing the sunny side, too...

Another issue that requires balance in making good decisions is being wary *not to get stuck in all the difficulty* of decision making. This means not getting bogged down in the usual negatives which surround making decisions.

decision: by original 15ᵗʰ century definition, means *a cutting off.* In other words, when we possess a thought that demands a choice between two or more variables, we mentally must *cut off* (separate) which of our options is best. In so doing, our decision is made.

Because making up our minds has a lot to do with addressing the negative we associate with decision making, our *decision making emphasis* can largely reside there—*in* that negative.

For example:

"If I retire at 62, I'll may miss my friends, lose my identity, probably not exercise either my body or my brain, be a pain to my wife even though she now says she'd like me home with her, wish I hadn't retired...", and so on.

In the above paragraph, the focus is on all the things *we hope to avert* in our decision making, on whether or not to retire at 62. They are all valid considerations, but only reveal half the story.

Addressing only the negative possible outcomes of our decision skews our ultimate decision making ability; it's lop-sided.

Instead of continually dwelling on making all the moves to avoid negative that can potentially occur, if we *also* focus on the positive outcomes of retiring at 62, we add needed balance supporting the final decision:

"If I retire now, what *good can come from it"?* Because our emotional outlook so heavily influences feeling and decision making, without positive vision and hope as impetus, the very decision to proceed may well lack initiative to do so, due to preoccupation with all the avoidance of the negative we so try to achieve.

Some positives about retiring at 62 might include:

- having time to genuinely focus on important things
- accurately perceiving retirement as being a new beginning, an invitation for personal growth
- having my horizons broadened, helping not only myself but others
- being a real aid and helper to my wife, bettering our relationship
- enhancing health—less of life's heavy career demands reduce blood pressure and stress, making me easier to live with, compared to the years of career pressure.

The list could go on, but the idea here is to *hold as fast to the positive elements of decisive issues as we do the negative.*

Making actual written lists of pros & cons, although rudimentary, is more effective than not doing so:

- Get it all down on paper; start a value prioritization of the elements. Weed out the lesser important, bit by bit, and witness the remaining evidence for a good decision beginning to emerge.

*5. Get the facts (the truth), but **avoid** needless rabbit trails*

This is about mind focus, limitations, and boundaries. Nothing will cloud the decision making process more than a tangential, not central, thought coming to mind and creating a new rabbit trail for concentration.

Idea *overload and pursuit only dilutes emphasis* of the base, key elements. Confusion is created, hampering ability of distinguishing between what's important and what isn't.

When young, I hunted rabbit and pheasant. I can remember—amid low-growing, briary thickets of underbrush—rabbit trails crossed and intersected in what appeared to me a maze of confused configuration! How on earth, I'd ask myself, does that rabbit have any idea where he would be at any point in time?

Maybe that quagmire of what seemed to be random pathways serves rabbits well. But it doesn't humans, who have capacity far greater than rabbit-reason. Rabbits appear to have three main reasoning capacities: forage for food, avoid hunters, and reproduce.

Although human reasoning has highly complex capacity, that volume can actually get in the way if rabbit trails aren't held in check. To counter straying idea pursuits:

- Force prioritization—*stay with the topic at hand.*
- Follow-through—accomplish some analysis of the current priority before undertaking another, but not to the point analysis becomes obsessive. It's never possible to cover and check out ALL aspects of any given issue, so learning to know where to begin and back off analytical research is both advantageous and wise. No one can dot every 'i' and cross every 't'. In other words: pursue factual truth, reject what's false, and then go on to the next priority topic on the list.

Intuitive or Analytical Decision Making: Which is best?

INTUITION-BASED DECISIONS

This chapter began by stating most everything we do on a daily basis involves decision making. Most of those hundreds of judgments (problem solving techniques) involve the intuitive form of decision making.

Intuitive thought has other names: quick guesses, gut feelings, hunches, snap judgments, sixth sense, hasty decisions, and guesses. Many of these sorts of decisions are simple, relatively unimportant, and originate through habit formation, good or bad.

Not all intuitive decisions, however, are unimportant. Sometimes urgent circumstances demand them; other times offering a 'good enough' type answer originates with intuition.

Have you ever had a decision just—pop up, seemingly from nowhere? That's intuition as well. Intuitions may also develop, consciously or not, from personal observations over a period of time. Intuition depends largely on accumulated information you've taken in, the source of which, if you had to define it, would be largely unnoticed and unremembered—maybe wholly unconscious in origin.

Intuitive thinking enables you to unconsciously utilize hundreds, maybe thousands of bits and pieces of knowledge you possess in memory. In these situations, your mind functions fast, *without any realization of a detailed review of a process of analytical reasoning*. In seconds you can have a leap of understanding or it can warn you, encourage you, provide an answer or inkling, a criticism, a prediction, an idea, or a solution.

ANALYTICALLY-BASED DECISIONS

The type of decision making described earlier in this chapter (whether or not to retire at 62) is of the analytical variety, not the intuitive.

Analytical reasoning is far more complex and procedural than intuitive reasoning. It more involves logic, thought-through content, and often sequential thinking. Actual life experience isn't central to thinking analytically because everything is based on analyzing actual word and thought based data.

SO, WHAT'S THE BEST REASONING METHOD IN MAKING IMPORTANT LIFE DECISIONS?

Retirement and aging decisions draw from both intuitive and analytical reasoning sources, but a distinction between the two is important to be noted:

To make good decisions going into life's last third, a *substantial* intuitive skill base (thinking skills) is important because it presents learned experience skills acquired over the course of life. Some examples of this learned skill base are:

- an acquired, extensive body of knowledge
- a learned ability to distinguish between relevant and irrelevant ideas
- a variety of experience memories and accurate interpretation of them
- memory of other peoples' experiences and accurate interpretation of what was witnessed
- a degree of emotional stability
- a relative freedom from relying on biases—and *hopefully* a measure of acquired wisdom thrown in for good measure!

In the paragraph above, I emphasized the importance of possessing a *substantial* intuitive skill base. If we don't have, or haven't developed a good degree of these skills by the time we're nearing retirement, we lack an important contributive component of good judgment and decision making as we look to later life.

The good news, however, is that most all boomers possess some degree of these important life attributes; obviously—the more the better.

Suggestion: As you scan the list of intuitive skills listed, know that it's not too late to be reinforcing the content of each.

Think on each of the six listed skills, doing a mental inventory of where you stand in each of the categories. Just by reading and mulling over these important intuitive characteristics, *you jog awareness in your thinking* of their need. That awareness will then likely stimulate *more* awareness of these skills in everyday experiences. In short, it's never too late to continually sharpen mind skills!

Intuitive skills are important because they *form a foundation* for important *analytical* decision making. What we're dealing with here is not an "either/or", but a "both/and" arrangement. The better equipped we are in the intuitive base, the better we can implement strong analytical abilities.

There's also an interesting reciprocity here: the more we exercise analytical decision making, the greater our intuitive skills are developed. One feeds the other; kind of a win-win situation.

What much of this comes down to is that *soberly exercising* what's between our ears—be it of intuitive or analytical origins—continually increases our capacity to make quality decisions. It's the lethargic mind that atrophies; if we don't use it, we lose it, as the saying goes.

Why is getting the totality of our thinking skills in good order prior to retirement so important? Much of later life quality of living *depends* on it. The decisions made now in pre-retirement—regarding personal vision for and about post-career living—will affect daily experiences and life direction once we're there:

The scout motto…, remember? Be prepared.

WHAT YOU NEED TO KNOW:

- Possibly re-read this chapter. I've found that since I've written the chapter itself, I take even more pause in thinking-through criteria that I know commands sound decision making.
- Decision making is *continual* in daily living; therefore, the *need* to do so well!
- Learning to make better decisions can begin anytime. We all can stand an ever sharpening of decision-making skills.

14

The Paradox of Medical Progress and Physical Aging

ADDRESSED IN THIS CHAPTER:

- How medical progress directly impacts issues of living longer.
- As medicine advances, does it inadvertently deteriorate life?
- The mania for life extension—do we do ourselves a disservice?

Life is just plain full of paradox it seems. In Chapter 9, we witnessed how retirement and aging can be paradoxical. Now we'll chug through another of those quizzical, seeming impossible to solve life realities that deeply challenges not only our intellect and consciences, but our hearts as well.

Pit Stop Encouragement!

Before getting into another heavy topic, I'd like to provide what I hope is encouragement to stay with me in this reading journey. *This entire first section of the book is about as uplifting as most of the sobering life reality content it conveys!* I want to reassure you, by the time we're done you will be edified, positive, and have a lilt in your step as you continue your personal walk toward retirement.

Much more to come. . .

Questions of Life and Death

Up to this point, we've been looking at life processes all of which, in one way or another, will impact you and me sometime in our retirements. The content in this and the next chapter are possibly the heaviest in the entire book.

Ultimately, as life reality affects some circumstance in our lives where committed decisions need to be made, it is my sincere hope that our time together here may have provided at least a strand of positive help or insight for that possible eventuality—for you and for me. (Each line I write is a reminder I need to put into practice my own words....)

When we find ourselves having to deal with what can often be anguishing decision making, we are up against that old and difficult bugaboo—making up our minds based on knowledge and wisdom, not being persuaded by emotion.

Emotion plays into most, if not all, major decisions, but is not to be the decision maker.

This chapter will present *tough situations that challenge personal ethics, beliefs, and real-life circumstances.*

But first let's reinforce the need of

- recognizing undesired or unpleasant life reality needs to be as forthrightly confronted as reality to which we're easily drawn (the Pleasure Principle)
- getting ourselves *moving,* not whining, seeking out the best information pathway we can that will help in sound decision making in later years
- realizing there are no 'stop & go lights' in difficult, remote life areas. The better prepared we are ahead of time, when those troublesome crossroads are encountered, the more conditioned our minds will be to at least to stop, look and listen before pulling out blindly into the intersection!

So many people ignore, put off, or even more commonly, just put on blinders and cover their ears to the unattractive, raucous parts of living that offend human sensitivities. I know we've gone through this earlier, but it is so important that we own up to reality, even when we don't want to, repetition from a new slant may be helpful.

Earlier, Jack Lalanne was mentioned. Let's set up a quick hypothetical comparison to illustrate the importance of having courage to *face and decide*, when it's easier to avert.

A good example between facing and shucking reality is Jack Lalanne versus a make-believe acquaintance—let's call him 'Chip' (as in potato)—an overweight, under-exercised, indifferent, stressed out, mentally unstimulated couch potato. (Okay, he's a nice guy and all, but needs a fire lit where the sun don't shine!)

One of the two men in this comparison, Lalanne, made a choice long ago, in his teens, to not be sickly and weak (actual fact). The other fellow made an even much later in life choice, having had more life experience at that point than LaLanne had as only a teen, to plop and let TV mentality do his thinking, even providing some decision making for him.

Even as far back as LaLanne's early adulthood, obtaining information is not difficult. That said, both these fellows had solid, life-reality information available concerning the physical body and good health. Notice the difference between these two men:

LALANNE

(the following is a direct quote from a "Jack LaLanne" search, Wikipedia.org)

> LaLanne wrote that as a boy he was addicted to sugar and junk food. At age 15, he heard Paul Bragg give a talk on health and nutrition. Bragg's message had a powerful influence on LaLanne, who **decided** (my emphasis) to focus on his diet and exercise habits. He studied Henry Gray's Anatomy of the Human Body and concentrated on bodybuilding and weightlifting.

CHIP, THE COUCH POTATO

Our 60 year old friend, however, didn't have Paul Bragg as inspiration, but that's irrelevant; likely, over the years he's had ten times the informational input originally available to LaLanne. But it's been ignored, put off, or his Pleasure Principle sensitivities have been offended—that is, *it's really all too much trouble.* So Chip becomes his own self-fulfilling prophecy; i.e., he set a course not to pursue something as important as health and personal welfare, and now lives as physical representation of that poor decision judgment.

I ask you, my reader: When it comes to gaining information that can urge you toward quality later-life planning, are you willing to confront reality with that information, and then do what it takes to establish prudent life choices (as did LaLanne)? Or, instead, will you bask in the illusion that personal comfortability of money, leisure, and having no genuine life purpose will be your sufficiency as the years move on?

Ever-advancing Medicine

Applying our timeline tool, who cannot say it's simply *wonderful*, from a medical care standpoint, to live in America in the current day; we are the envy of the world!

Push our timeline cursor backwards, however to, say, days of the American Revolution, and we see the chances of living to what we now consider old age to be have been only a pipedream. Early Americans rarely, if ever, had the luxury of *living long enough to experience* the miseries associated with genuine old age and its cousins, ever-increasing physical and mental decline.

Think of it: George Washington reportedly complained of his wooden teeth never fitting well. It's said pliers worked well on the originals as long as they weren't so badly decayed they crumbled. Sounds like fun, doesn't it? Novocain would have been a handy addition to the pliers, don't you think?

Most people *never accumulated enough years* to get into what we know as stages of frailty, feebleness, and extended debility. Medical assistance and achievement was in its infancy, which meant infant mortality rates soared, while grown men literally worked themselves to death.

Imagine! An average, pre-revolutionary father/husband, with saw and axe in hand, built his house by cutting his own timber, made them into logs, then erected the house and fireplace; oh, once the land had been cleared of stumps and all. As he'd be doing all this, he had to gather enough firewood for the upcoming winter to survive the cold. Then the following spring, gardens—of not the Martha Stewart variety—*had* to succeed, livestock needed to be bred and slaughtered. And hopefully preserved. Obesity wasn't much of a problem in early America.

Meanwhile, mothers/wives were driven equally as hard in caring for the never-ending domestic responsibilities of home and child rearing: dishwashers?, washing machines?, flushing toilets?—are you kidding? Utilizing the posterior defecating mechanism properly situated in yon, non air-conditioned outhouse was more like it! On a hot and humid summer day, you sat and counted the number of spiders crawling about; in winter, you planned on quick evacuation in that outdoor freezer, in more ways than one. Running water? It sure did, but you had to fetch it first.

On and on it went. When time came to deliver new life, the pregnant, gentler gender may have been the toughest soul on the homestead! Death probability, due to medical childbirth complications, to her and to the child, tested the strongest of womanly character and tenacity.

Thomas Jefferson, as reported in the *Jeffersonian Cyclopedia* states, when asked if he had life to do over again, would he. He said he would, but eloquently qualifies its longevity, indicating he'd have no desire to live before twenty-five, or after sixty. Quoting his reasons for eliminating the old age period he states: *For the latter period, with most of us, the powers of life are sensibly on the wane, sight becomes dim, hearing dull, memory constantly enlarging its frightful blank and parting with all we have ever seen or known, spirits evaporate, bodily debility creeps on palsying every limb, and so faculty after faculty quits us, and where then is life?* (Jeffersonian Cyclopedia, p. 505, entry #4759-Life)

Have recent generations, especially ours, been blessed with medical miracles?

The current (2011) political machinery in Washington, however, concerning the future of American healthcare is, in the best of descriptions, undergoing transition. You may read this book in 2011, 2021, or whenever. I wonder today what we, if we're around, will experience as fallout from current political decisions manifest in years to come. Unfortunately, there is clear writing on the wall, circumventing much guesswork of speculation.

The crux of modern medicine is certainly about people, not political machinery. Although medical advances greatly serve us, we, ironically, are also saddled with the tag-along, negative ramifications that accompany such advancement. Continued below, we examine some powder keg reality, a pre-detonation peek at irrefutable facts only blindness could miss.

The Deepening Healthcare Quagmire

Frankly, we have a boiling pot of healthcare stew on the stove, and I don't know that anyone is around to keep an eye on the gas burner, as it were. If the pot boils over, scald, pain, destruction, hyper-mess will all occur. And that's assuming the *gas* isn't eventually shut off due to political, economic ineptitude and insanity.

Newton rightly said of the physical universe, *"To every action there is always opposed an equal reaction."* Such principle is truly universal, applying as well to societal and individual applications.

Here's the core of the problem, and wherein the paradox of medical progress lies: The ever-increasing life extensions medicine creates through scientific advances, all with mankind's welfare in mind—at the same time—*means we live longer in states of debilitation!* The physical frame *has to* progressively die. Modern medicine, because it has prolonged life, *also* prolongs precisely what we dread—increasing duration of progressing disability.

I'm sorry, but that old acquaintance—reality—is again staring us in the face. Jefferson didn't like this old-age thing, nor did the wealthy business executive in an earlier chapter. My own mother told me not to get old, and I never said in this writing any of this aging stuff is easy. What have we created?

Medical Miracles—Friend or Foe?

It gets more complicated.

A SOCIETY OF THE AGED

The average life expectancy of Americans, as of 2010, is about seventy-eight years. In the early 1900's it was about forty-five. The over eighty-five octogenarians can claim to be in the fastest growing age category of all. At the same time, birth rates continue to fall, meaning Gen X and Y will be burdened with heavier than ever fiscal responsibility to fund Medicare and Medicaid—to say nothing of the "perfect financial storm" that, as of this writing, is likely to occur.

The financial storm and the societal storm may well combine to form a mega-storm. Costs for medical care have to continue to increase because we live longer and longer. The longer we live, the greater the debilitation, so the greater the costs to keep us alive.

Let he with eyes to see realize—within the next several decades, getting older won't be getting easier. All the more reason to develop late-life game plans – now. If we hem and haw, not deciding to get some solid, personal, pre-retiree planning in order, waiting until the probable storms hit to do so, we'll be like idiots on the Titanic's deck pondering or arguing about which deck chair to sit on instead of heading for lifeboats!

I may be criticized and branded "Chicken Little", meaning I worry too much, things aren't that bad, the government will take care of us, things always get better, don't think about the bad stuff, eat, drink, be merry. I report what I see; you decide.

What *Have* We Created?

Advanced, scientific technology is not the key that perpetuates real life. It has proven to extend years, but in our insistence of living forever, the aged are finding, bluntly, it may have been better to have died earlier of diseases that are now under control, than to languish in ever advancing physical and mental deterioration, which in no way can be averted as genuine old age takes its toll. Have we shot ourselves in the proverbial foot?

To analyze the situation further, we find we may have created a Frankenstein 'type' of old age. Dare I say *unnatural* life extension has created intense problematic conditions that will probably intensify as time goes on?

It's Not About Ungratefulness

Above I use the word *unnatural* referring to life, regardless of its quality, being pushed further and further into calendar years.

Is increasing life span right or wrong; natural, or pushing the unnatural?

It's like debating what's normal and what's not. The logical crux of the matter lies, of course, in what and whose standard is used as the benchmark for normality. Establishing a universal standard on some thoughts or entities, about which everybody can be happy, is like trying to anchor a rolling canon on a pitching deck in a hurricane—impossible. Just where is the 'right' anchor point to lash the canon? And who makes that decision? Based on what? My subjectivity or yours?

That I not be misconstrued, I, as well as we a nation collectively, are certainly thankful, or should be, for the ills cured by modern medicine! To this day, yet in safe keeping, remains a small, metal, sort of lapel pin I was given in elementary school in 1954. The pin is a child's reward and significant memento for being part of the Salk vaccine implementation (Jonas Salk), preventing polio. It reads

*Polio Pioneer–1954 The National Foundation for
Infantile Paralysis.*

In the last twenty years, I've had three major surgical
procedures, two of which have relieved severe back pain,
and the other removing cancer. Do I applaud the modern
medicine? Certainly! But herein illustrates my point on
what such advances have also created. Had I not had the
benefit of cancer removal, I might be dead today, nine years
later. But here I am, and may so be for a decade or two,
maybe more, to come.

What do we do with this situation? Is all this good or bad?
Right now, I'm glad to have been delivered from the deadly
killer. Had I lived even fifty years earlier, with no early detec-
tion, I probably wouldn't have had the option to venture into
being 'aged'. Now, suppose I live to seventy-eight or eighty-
eighty, and at that point have to have someone, if that one is
indeed available, change my diapers, feed me, make my decisions, put up with fractured memory, be a burden to others,
and God only knows what else!

It's difficult to contemplate, "Oh, you won't be a burden,
we love you." Thank God I'm loved, but of course I'll be a burden—certainly a physical one, likely a mental one, and if my
family is involved in the care, definitely an emotional burden
as well.

This has nothing to do with being loved or not, but concerns senescence—what can be viewed as many small, incre-
mental dying events on the way toward the last breath. Uplifting stuff, isn't it?

Gerontology suggests many, maybe millions of senescent
individuals are, even today, experiencing an internal, sometimes vocal, wish that they'd passed away earlier.

I'm not attempting to make a pro or con case here, but am
only relating what I've seen and have been told by aged individuals, to say nothing of such evidence being demonstrated
in countless nursing homes and public print. The plain truth
is not exaggerated.

And the simple, profound paradox continues: as medicine
advances, it inadvertently deteriorates life.

WHAT YOU NEED TO KNOW:

- The whole of the life extension topic is so highly individual, I believe I'm incapable of speaking to this issue amid anyone's life but my own.

15

Challenges to Morality and Ethics—Keeping Things in Balance

ADDRESSED IN THIS CHAPTER:

- Ethics and morality—how they play into life extension.
- The negative accompanying medical advances
- Tough societal issues

Ripe Old Age

There's no one among us who would want to revert back to the tyranny of diseases now under control. For example, sky high infant mortality, plagues, and my own run-in with cancer—that place where, at one time, it's mere mention issued an indictment of certain death, often in short order.

Modern medicine is wonderful! We live in the golden age of the Golden Years—to a point....

Bringing it up to date, who would want to terminate finding a cure for the premier nastiness of Alzheimer's, a demon of individual and family wrecking to the nth proportion. Victims often can't control elimination, must be fed and bathed, lose self cognizance and control, experience episodes of inordinate rage and so on. May the cure be close at hand so victims can live to the proverbial "ripe old age"!

"Ripe old age" is the point of focus here, not the needed cure of an awful disease. More precisely, old age (translated 'extended' age) can be "ripe", but because as a society we strive for life-indefinite, *are we pushing ripe to the spoiling stage?*

Metaphorically, let's consider "ripe" as connected to the fullness of fruit maturation—the summer peach being a good example (also a good time to lighten-up a bit!). We can liken our fully matured selves to a peach having reached its zenith in the orchard—just tickle it with the fingers to have it fall, wonderfully tasty, into an outstretched hand.

I grow peaches. The time to pick them for best eating is *just* before they are ready to fall from the limb. That's why tickling them works so well. This gentle prompting drops the fruit into the hand, just prior to it releasing itself and falling to the ground where bruising is possible.

Peaches fall, *naturally,* as part of their design for reproducing themselves, not to only taste good in mid-summer. Left to itself on the ground, and with soil contact, the peach quickly rots. Later, the outer pit cracks open, releasing the seed of life, which also makes soil contact. If allowed to germinate; behold, a new tree is born.

Unnaturally, the peach could be held to the tree interminably, I suppose, by an apparatus of some sort. It could be taped, wired, maybe glue applied to the stem's tree connection; maybe even cut the limb off with the peach attached so it wouldn't become disconnected from the only life it's known! There are lots of inventive ways we could *prevent the peach's detachment from life*—the tree upon which it's grown.

But spoiling on the tree, unnaturally, would produce an offense to the peach itself, countering natural processes. Programmed to die, it would, in fact stink, ooze, rot, and eventually be cast off in a form of total decadence—worthless to provide nourishment to humans.

Modern life-sustainment through medical advances comes with a peculiar set of problems, similar to artificially keeping the peach attached to the tree. Mankind can contravene natural law, but not without repercussions.

145

Just as the cycle of fruit production can be interrupted, have we altered, in the name of life extension, human life flow? I don't attempt to support or criticize the outcomes stemming from extended life created by scientific medical advances. Bringing the subject to the forefront, however, causes us to be continually aware that as we face the longer lives we're creating, our society needs to make provision for the alteration. And if society won't, how will you, personally? This is an intensifying, perplexing problem.

ENTER: ETHICS AND MORALITY

Ultimately, we are forcing entry of the hand of conscience, beliefs, morality, social ethics, even legalities. The Terri Schiavo case is landmark, involving an extremely incapacitated woman's husband removing her feeding tube that had kept the woman alive for years. Legal battles raged, families were split, and an American culture came face to face with a situation brought on partially by advanced technology. This harrowing experience has put critical focus on the implication of medical advances spilling over into where we really live—the right and wrong, good and bad of it all—and how to make the best of what we likely can't change.

ENTER: 2011 AND BEYOND.
WHERE ARE WE GOING WITH ALL THIS?

Through advancing medical technology and understanding, we learn to better, and preserve to an extent, human health with our mechanical and biological tinkering of the human frame. At the same time, though, the added longevity can not only backfire, it *challenges our core values* on how to handle it.

Difficult questions come into play as technology's influence forces such issues of deep consideration to the forefront. We find ourselves face to face with questions such as:

- What's life all about?
- Why are we here in the first place?
- Why do we have that sense something's not quite right with some of mankind's seemingly moral decisions?

• Why are our consciences pricked by sacred (I don't mean religious) concepts of 'to live or to die'.

Digging deeper—

• Why do we have consciences, anyway—that innate sense that certain things are inherently right and wrong?
• Is it the result of some primordial slime *realizing* the need for moral parameters to perpetuate itself, so it evolved an abstract entity we call conscience? Many would have us so believe.
• Where do we, as a people, set our parameters on the extent to which we *puuuush* the perpetuation of, need I say, the *mortal* human frame? These earthly bodies categorically have limits; death is certain.

Questions such as these are as piercing and without common agreement and solution as are those deepest queries of why we age and die, a topic gingerly touched upon earlier.

We live in a world that increasingly denies the existence of absolutes, which contributes nicely to getting one's own way, but not to an overall good. As some attempt to dispense with any standard to which man is accountable, then "my view is as good as your view". This approach sounds good and is politically correct, but leads to an ideological quagmire—each man does what best aligns with personal desire and subsequent viewpoint. That can lead to pandemonium, even war—on many levels.

As no universal standard seems possible and acceptable to all on this earthly plane, most civil men, in attempt to live in relative peace, keep the ideological tenets of life in continual debate, ever floating in a sea of flux and abeyance. And life's syncopated beat continues.... And the cannon on the pitching deck slams, and breaks, and never gets anchored.

In the best of times, mankind agrees to disagree; in the worst, we kill each other.

Although I'd love to get into it all, our journey here isn't an attempt in unraveling life's more complex queries. The more awareness of life's complexities we possess, however, the greater our ability to view the entire life picture and assess our personal relationship to it. From there, increased personal ability toward *good life decision making* is presented.

And *that* is the substance of our journey together.

The Negative Accompanying Medical Advances

HEALTH ISSUES

Medical advances have created an old age life segment evermore perpetuated by an extended time of enduring debilitation, feebleness, and a greater propensity toward deep level dementia. Remember the Colonists? They rarely had to worry about such things!

AGE ISSUES

Second, the aging population will skyrocket as boomers, at the current rate of about ten thousand per day, retire for the next eighteen years (Boomer births within the 1946–1964 period).

Buckle up; bumpy ride ahead! This explosion 'officially' began January 1, 2011. These figures are estimates only, but tell us we're into *millions* of 'life-extended' retirees coming on board within the next two decades, a large portion of whom are certain to live past the quality of life threshold, and into general and increased feebleness because of senescence, that ever increasing deterioration accompanying growing old.

INCREASED COST ISSUES

Third, rising costs are certain to progressively increase hardships to anyone requiring lengthy, ongoing care. Assistance with even the most basic of life necessities can be required *for years, if not decades*—feeding and elimination, to say nothing of certain need for overall observation and care.

CAREGIVER ISSUES

The necessity of this care will increasingly demand personal involvement of the caregiver.

Amid all the insensitivities modern culture has created, family, fortunately, yet remains. In the past, the very elderly were usually cared for within the family unless health deterioration worsened beyond the family's care giving capabilities. Usually, death came earlier than it does today. Fortunately, strong family ties still do exist, but are strained as divorce, multiple family marriages, same-sex marriages, and the unmarried free-for-all increase in frequency and intensity.

Crucial: Major cultural shifts due to economic pressure will force loved ones into the difficult position of having to care for the elderly by means of not working. This may create undo financial hardship on individual families as income is also sorely needed. Our debt-ridden economy will increasingly tax John Q. Taxpayer, so not working, assuming there are jobs, won't be an option. Outside the family, professional care giving may be an option if home coffers are full enough to support it, but this is not often the case in middle income bracket households.

"We have a problem, Houston!"

As the elder population mushrooms in the next couple of decades, *care givers—meaning the family relative, the professional, the government, or all three combined*—will be facing the mountain swell of a geriatric society needing care. The balloon can only stretch so far—something will have to give. Society is almost certain to be forced into position to bend the rules somewhere; it's that "somewhere" that is particularly worrisome.

How might this all play out? Of course, consciences of reasonably moral people find it difficult to negate the worth of human life, regardless of age and condition, but the more frail life becomes as age increases, which heaps prolonged misery upon the aged soul, the more acutely agonizing becomes the emotional predicament on behalf of the care giver, as well as an increased operational moral dilemma for society as a whole:

- Conscience and compassion don't want to perpetuate growing misery upon the ebbing life already bound by machines and drugs.
- Conscience, again, kicks in and blocks what the heart really feels (emotion): that the poor soul 'should' be released from what seems to be interminable anguish and torment.

So vividly comes to mind a dignified old woman, in her early nineties, maybe, at Pennswood Village. She told me privately how she so wished she could die, alleviating personal physical pain, the continual nagging that she was the "only one left" of family and friends, and the never changing presence of the reality of it all glaring at her continually. She went on to say that the care, which she obviously had been able to afford, had been wonderful, but *"why do I have to live so long!?"* were her words.

The paradox continues; the better the care, the longer the period of enduring the ever-increasing frequency of the slowness of dying, until the end finally comes.

WHAT'S A GEN X-ER TO DO?

The mixture of all this is, at the very least, difficult. Gen-X'ers will be dealing with the 'infection' of a new social pathology:

- The need for social support must dramatically increase because of the increased volume of the elderly.
- More elderly mean more bed pan changes, a poor paying job.
  - Because of poor pay, there will be less young people filling the unglamorous duties of daily elder care.
- Governmental, universal elder care is likely because needs won't be met by supply and demand principles.
  - Big government always yields small returns- a truism.
  - What turns out to be an anemic, old age health 'care' program equates to a rationing of care from already questionable government tactics—depending on who's running the government.

- Individual families, in order to supplement poor state run care, will suffer the decision between being home to provide needed elder care, or continuing working to provide for their own family.

The scenario listed above certainly isn't a concrete prediction, but unless I'm prematurely senile, it at least provides a probable outline of society's elder care infrastructure in decades to come.

Anything can change, but considering the current (2011) projected inter-relationships of expected elder care volume, Wall Street instability, what goes on within the Washington Beltway, and the overall, general moral deterioration of society, can much more be expected?

A Crumbling Foundation

Moral deterioration? Likely I'll get rebuttals on this one. Nevertheless:

Our nation, as a whole, has been slowing wearing away the Judeo-Christian notion and foundation that *our time on earth is constructed,* by God, *of set seasons of life, paralleling nature's own.* Please hear me out before I'm relegated to not being with the times, or a quasi-religious nut case. This is not about *religion,* but simply about life as we know it. Indeed, all major world religions acknowledge the cycle of life.

It can be argued that all life extension is doing is putting off the end, which is true, *but at what expense?* Well, I said in the previous chapter this topic is too big for more depth here; guess I better stick with that....

Knitting it together:

- We love youthfulness—don't want to see it, or life, end.
- We hate the ravages of illness and disease.
- Medical advancements offer highly worthy stop-gap measures.
- But we can't live forever.

- The so-called and ubiquitous catch phrase "healthy living"—*in terms of the aging reality*—eventually becomes inapplicable, even silly, as ultimate body deterioration inevitably sets in: I mean—cars *do* wear out, don't they? There comes a point when the body and mind *are done*. There's a season to be born, live, die—done. Spring, fall, summer, winter—done. We need to stop avoiding the unpleasant presence and absolute reality of life's termination point, realizing *'the car ultimately must run its last tank of gas'*.
- The presence of life's finality is certainly a strain on loving care, conscience, and what's best. Playing God isn't ours to do, but where are the lines, as it were? Compromise, rationalization, genuine sincerity—all these are integrated and challenged as we deal with death of the physical frame, especially for those we love, or for our own.

Disposal Mentality—the Slippery Slope

A slippery slope, that hackneyed phrase I've avoided in this writing, is so outright applicable here; it's precisely where American society finds itself in terms of what to do with the whole of later-life.

During our book journey, later-life is a term used to describe both the retirement phase and the progressing aging phenomenon under which retirement falls.

We *began* with retirement being the book's central theme and *will end* there as well—positively; making the very best of life's good and bad entanglements.

But amid good planning and intentions, life reality and declining morality suggest an increasingly traction-less slope. Are we "… glidin' down the highway… or slip-slidin' away", as Paul Simon astutely observed in another regard?

Where the aging dilemma is headed becomes more and more troubling as the probability of lesser care giving ability increases.

As the years mount, the *sheer volume* of elderly health demands will increasingly demand *unprecedented care needs, likely beyond the scope of adequate supply.*

Where the slope appears to be offering the least traction, however, is the direction of society's ethical compass, *ever heading away from highly esteeming the elderly, and instead toward—I hate to say it—a forward creeping, disposal mentality.* This advance is slow, but as the many aforementioned conditions intensify, what will shift this course of social calamity?

I'm *not* saying there's a conspiracy afoot to bring on death by decree. We don't need a totalitarian dictator, corrupt government, or morally void societal perspective to cause trouble. Instead, we have our innocent—and *otherwise* beneficial—medical technology, linked to our preoccupation with youth and living forever, greasing the channel of one already oil-slick, slippery slope.

With our modernity has arisen a deep-level shift *from* the centuries-old maxim that our elderly are the respected culmination of life's natural flow.

This has even been well sited in pop culture: The Byrds song of the '60s, *Turn, Turn, Turn,* and Bruce Springsteen's more recently released version both, dare I make mention, find their secular inspiration in the so astute biblical narrative found in the Book of Ecclesiastes.

Needless to say, purposely striving to achieve balance and traditional morality, as our society experiences dramatic changes in aging, is an unprecedented challenge. Warp speed increases in technology, a waning emphasis on once held sacredness of things that really matter, a watering down adherence to spiritual absolutes—all these life realities are powerfully active in American societal culture.

Point blank, there is no apparent blanket solution to the ever-increasing dilemma of increased aging—individually, or as an entire society. It's a fact of life to be maturely addressed and understood. From that gained awareness, good decision making, planning, and moral responsibility must become the underpinnings of any genuine heading toward societal sanity.

WHAT YOU NEED TO KNOW:

- Determine your stand on pushing life to the timeline limit. Let those close to you know your feelings. Be certain to have your feelings in writing via a Living Will, etc.

- Suggestion: If you feel strongly about the sacredness of aging, and that it should be maintained, let your voice be heard. In other cultures, especially those of the East, elders are highly honored. From my public circulation and observations, I see the opposite prevalent in America. As ugly as the term is—"disposal mentality", is a scourge on American soil and should be countered as best possible.

- The problems are real, and sensitively caring for everyone is an elusive dream. But we shouldn't acquiesce to evils and negatives among us; rather, as is possible, overcome evil with good.

16

Change & Transition

ADDRESSED IN THIS CHAPTER:

• Change and transition are not synonymous terms.
• Transition is a three-stage process.

This chapter does just what its title implies; it makes a "change" in our focus, causing us to "transition" into new arenas of thought and direction that will take us into the center of retirement preparation on several practical levels. We've been discussing the importance of personally preparing now for retirement and dealing with continuing aging and even life extension.

We understand:

• the complexity of retirement and aging are much more involved than meets the eye
• the need to not limit retirement perception to the money/leisure mentality so promoted by our culture
• we can't minimize or ignore later-life's difficulties. Instead, we confront them, choosing to seek out pearls of good amid the negative quagmire. Later-life, indeed, possesses pearls of value, somewhat as do oysters. The meat of oysters obscure pearls within, just as the effects of aging tend to hide the beauty of our true personal value—our inner person.

To summarize some broad concepts, we've spent time:

- *Learning to create* sound decision making, centered in living in the 'today' of life, not in the yesterdays.
- *Getting the mind to choose* thought patterns that both address genuine aging difficulties and provide as reasonable, beneficial life solutions as possible.
- *Finding realistic ways to turn* aging negative into practical good—
  - *learning* to create...
  - *getting* the mind to choose...
  - *finding* realistic ways to turn... (you might fill in the blanks...).

Note there is *activity* involved in each phrase above; something *we* must do—

- *learning to create*
- *getting the mind to choose*
- *finding realistic ways to turn difficulty into at least less difficulty, neutrality, or perhaps genuine good!*

In short, each phrase is centered in 'moving' us from one place of *thinking* to another. *Do keep that "moving" thought in mind...*

Whenever an action of moving ahead—physically or mentally—is performed, two things happen:

- something past or old is left behind
- something new replaces it.

An example would be the animal kingdom's chimpanzee navigating the jungle. This small brute typifies the way we must often navigate life. As the chimp swings from vine to vine, his forward direction is advanced.

As the chimp advances through the jungle, and as we move from one stage of life to another, however, something not so obvious and simple occurs in each instance:

- In order to move forward, we must *release* something in order to grasp something else:

We release decades of career life in order to seize retirement.

The above sentence is a broad simplification of what happens during the migration of any life stage to the next; for example, moving from adolescence into adulthood, or being single to raising a family. Both instances involve a definite shift *from* one way of life *to* another.

The shift isn't necessarily quick, but is definitive, delivering powerful, unavoidable impact on our lives.

Change and Transition Aren't Synonymous

Today's retirement heavily centers on change and its companion, transition. Most folks think shifting away from the career way of life to one of retirement implies making a change or transition, the two words usually being thought of as different words for the same idea.

In part, this is true. We think of changing (transitioning) from one job to another, or making a career transition (change). But the two aren't the same; *transition is a function of change, and there's good reason to understand the distinction between the two:*

- **Change**—*an outward circumstance,* or group of them, *that makes a situation in life very different*: going away to college; getting married; getting divorced; losing a parent; being told you have terminal cancer; retiring!
- **Transition**—*an inward effect* in relation to the outward change of circumstances. *Transition is what we feel and how we react as result of the change in circumstances.* Change requires an inner adjustment that must be made to deal effectively with the altering of circumstances that occurs during the change. That inner adjustment is called transition.

Retirement creates an outward circumstance (change) that will have multiple effects on an individual's emotional and psychological outlooks (transition). Change is relatively simple compared to transition because change is easy to see and experience.

We leave the career, for example, and settle into a new mode of daily living. Probably home-life, recreational activities, relationships and much more will, in some degree, change. The emotional effects these changes create have to do with the transition that occurs inwardly.

Transition, conversely, involves this mental fallout *resulting from* the change; something to be experienced, inwardly, over time. Transition is about us inside—where we live—during a time requiring *psychological adjustment.* Not well adjusting during transition can have serious emotional impact that can cause maladjustment on many levels. Transition can be as remarkably good and fruitful as can it be negative. In cases of the latter, of course, needs to be dealt with carefully.

The 3-Parts of the Transition Process

Transition can be easy or difficult, depending on the individual, the circumstances of the change, or both. Transition isn't a one-time event, but occurs on a timeline. It possesses:
- a *beginning* (entering into whatever the change may be)
- a *mid-point* (where all the befuddlement and difficulty tends to develop and dwell)
- an *ending* (coming to a sense of arrival; i.e., settling in to the overall change having reduced the angst of the mid-point period.

I'm reminded of a descriptive section in one of Dr. James Dobson's excellent books on raising teens (hardly having to do with retirement!). The analogy he uses, although directed to what parents of teens usually undergo, so well applies to boomers who are changing from career to retirement life.

Dr. Dobson compares raising teens to launching a canoe in a river known for its changes in behavior (like raising children!):
- a *beginning* point of transition—launching a canoe into what appears a placid river (having children)
- a *mid-point*—encountering rapids, rocks, swiftly changing currents; i.e., potentially fearsome stuff! (teen years)

• an *ending*—emerging once again into calm water (children mature into early adulthood)

The change is taking the canoe trip; the transition is how we handle all the river run involves.

Nurturing, controlling, guiding adolescents from puberty to early twenties usually presents significant change for the parents just as migrating from years of career life to retirement presents to boomers. In retirement, we have the same time periods through which we must travel: a beginning, mid-point, and end; it's that ending with which we're really concerned because it's not so much how we start at retirement, but how we finish as we continue to age.

Ask yourself:

• Are you prepared for a 'canoe trip' into retirement?
• Watertight canoe?
• Helmet?
• Adequate flotation devices?
• Are you becoming aware that the retirement river has sections of turbulent rapids and protruding rocks?
• Are you counting on dodging them all instead of expending effort ahead of time for uncertain eventuality protection?

When you launch into retirement you are letting go of one thing in order to advance toward another, and need to consider preparation for the unknown:

change—letting go of shoreline safety for adventure in a river you've never navigated.

transition—what you'll face and how you'll deal with your new area of exploration.

WHAT YOU NEED TO KNOW:

• Change= switching from career to post-career living.
• Transition= a series of emotional/psychological events dealing with all the good and bad fallout resulting from making the major life change.

- Realize that *any* major life change will be accompanied by mainly emotional and psychological adjustment that takes transitional elements of time to process.

- Such realization performs a good check of personal emotional balance. It tends to emotionally evaluate and pace the 'move' from what has been to what now is.

17

Personal Identity Assessment

(Knowing Who We Are)

ADDRESSED IN THIS CHAPTER:

• Factors that shape identity.
• Questions that help us determine who we are.
• Careers can mask our core identity.

In Chapter 16, change and transition were defined and distinction made between the two. Also we established, as is customary throughout this book, that sensible preparedness for change, set in place now during the career phase of life, will probably make life easier later. If not easier, at least far ahead of what lack of preparation would, otherwise, involve!

Strengthening and resilience—two highly favorable life attributes, are by-products of preparation. If we are built-up, inwardly, we possess a confidence about our genuine, personal identity. Then, because of that confidence, we are enabled to better acclimate to life changes retirement and aging can bring. Changes *will* come and, remember, transitions will accompany each. To well handle the transitions we need a clear mental sight picture, strong inner fiber, and quality life values in which we deeply believe.

Knowing Our Real Self

We must know ourselves—*know* ourselves! Shakespeare was right on—"To thine own self be true." If we can't be brutally honest with self assessment, we aren't really in touch with who we are. Call it bull, horse pucky, manipulation, sour grape side-stepping—whatever the term; in short, if you live in *self-deception* you don't know the real you.

Indeed, façades and mental games can trick others. We can fool others much of the time because they can't see in our minds. Worse, we can fool our very selves! If we live to any degree in self deception and take that false self understanding into retirement; yes, and old age—when tough, real life thought decisions need to be made—*where will we look* inside for answers? To a synthetic or a genuine self? Which would you want; which would you trust? I'm talking about your own emotional, cognitive balance along with self understanding, and the ability to merge these toward quality decisions.

Please don't misunderstand me here. I'm not at all implying any of my readers live in self deception. To a degree, all humanity possesses some untruth within. We're all fallible; that's why Shakespeare admonishes to seek earnestly for self truth and reality.

If, therefore, we can agree on the necessity of going into retirement with strength and resilience of mind preparation (as much as is possible), let's look more carefully at this topic of how we currently define who we are.

All this can be plotted on the timeline of our lives. Broadly, please put yourself into the following questioning, addressing only what *you* can know of your personal identity:

- *Past*—Who have I been (not what did I do) during my career life?
  - What has been my character, my values?
  - What have been my most driving desires?
- *Current*—Am I that same person now as I near retirement, or do I have a different perception of self now that I'm older?
  - Do I see myself more honestly than when I was

younger; i.e., am I more sobered in self-appraisal than earlier on?
- If not, am I happy with what I see?
- *Future*—Am I, at my core, who I want to be when I retire? *That's* the big question. The heavy identity questions:
  - Do I know, in my heart of hearts, *who* I really am at this point in life, or do I live behind any façades, even unto myself?
  - Am I happy *with myself?*
  - Nitty-gritty: Am I the person, now, I want to be in retirement, or do I need to understand myself more honestly, completely, and possibly implement some changes?

Please don't feel at all intimidated or incriminated at such difficult questions. I've been there, too. I conveyed in the book's sub-title that *Wall Street & Main Street* won't offer much, if any, such fodder for the individual's consideration and personal development. Although I feel as a little "David", I believe I'm armed with smooth stones and a sling that can stand up to the Goliath of society's indifference, as it were… You can, too!

"To thine own self be true."

It's up to you and to me *to take ownership* of and for ourselves, *seek truth*, and become *sincerely honest with and about ourselves*. By so doing, we develop what I call *transitioning capacity*. Remember? Transitioning is the inner adjustment to the outward change.

Repeating two salient truths:

- Society, in general, *isn't interested in the inner you and your personal, genuine success at retirement life.*
- Many within the boomer culture personally *avoid* the hard questions of life, retirement, and aging due to the nasty influences of fear, ignorance, bias, neglect, and indifference.

Don't let those negatives or thin skin thwart your aims for *taking care of yourself!* Isn't that a reason you bought this book?

Societal culture may have the main chain of life well linked, but the personal *'you'* link is missing. It's around, somewhere—in your soul. Often it's fragmented or unclear, maybe not even acknowledged, but the substance of it all is always there.

We *can* piece this link into our personal life chain if we'll exercise objective, honest self inspection, resulting in establishing personal transitional strength for the change. This inner strength then can provide reasonable steadfastness, assurance, even happiness as we approach the autumn and winter life seasons ahead.

Part II will help all this develop.

Abstract Personal Identity; Practical Life Activity

Admittedly, considering abstract reality about our self perception isn't child's play. Further, to look inside often is difficult because subliminally, usually, we'd rather let lay in slumber deeper information about who we really are, the substance of which we may, or may not, be aware.

For instance, have you ever noticed how easy it is to basically ignore thinking deeply concerning who we are at our core being? Some might say "Who cares! I'm just me!" Others deeply contemplate their navels, so to speak, but ignore self examination for fear of kicking what might be a sleeping dog who doesn't like to be annoyed. Get the drift here? I'm saying—even if we're not particularly happy with who we think we are, it's often less painful to leave self-view alone than to risk potentially uncovering difficult reality about ourselves. (self-deception).

If, however, we are willing to pull off Mr. Shakespeare's admonition of being real with ourselves, we reap dividends in the practicality of daily living. In other words, we find life much more easy to acknowledge—life is good!

That's where we're headed with all this: *practical,* retirement living. To maximize practical retirement living means to finally release, for our good and that of those we touch, the true personhood each of us owns—our individual identity; our core being.

Careers Can Mask Our Core Identities

During most of our middle-age years, our core identity may have strongly shifted more than we think. Consider:

Our everyday life, for the last thirty-forty years, has been steered largely by career demands.

That's a broad stroke of the paint brush, but as we'll come to discuss, the strong impact and long duration of career life exerts powerful external pressures on the dreams, goals, passions, and desires we held dear, earlier in life.

Powerful external pressures force shifting of internal sensitivities.

Identity starts early in life. Identity is how we perceive ourselves at any given time. Genetics, and several life components, factor into the identity equation.

Beginning at infancy, life's events shape and solidify individual identity traits. Self-esteem is shaped as family, friends, and multiple life associations all combine in identity formation.

Whether or not we accurately perceive self by the time our career phase of life ends and retirement beckons, personal identity *has* been established. Our job, at that point in time, is to determine its genuineness and respond in the best ways possible.

The Anatomy of Career's Influence on Identity

This breakdown is designed to illustrate and support how vulnerable our personal identities are to strong, external career pressures over which we often have minimal control. In this context, career means the whole of money-producing work life: that necessary function we perform, which brings home the bacon.

Career is a huge, usually unrecognized organizer and steering mechanism; career is a central arena of life. Everyday practical living arenas involve broad, yet highly interrelated, areas of life we can term life circles, categories—or arenas.

Everything we do or think falls within one or more of these life arenas:

SIX LIFE ARENAS

1. Career

2. Family

3. Relationships

4. Self's relationship (two parts)
   • the abstract: self-esteem, self-regard, self appraisal
   • the physical: relating to use and care of the body

5. Spirituality

6. Leisure

Notice that *career* heads the list. There's a reason:

Career, during the decades-long chunk of our mid-life years, overarches, to various degrees, how the rest of life is conducted.

Dr. Richard Johnson, Ph.D., noted psychologist specializing in gerontology (effects of aging), and creator of the internationally applied Retirement Options program, uses the term "arenas". It's a good term. In Part II I'll be going much further into depth concerning the six life arenas:

They will help you begin to formulate your own plan toward the whole of retirement planning.

Career is the invisible dominator of most other life functions. This does not mean that career is more important or that it controls the other arenas, though it can. Its influence, however, on these other life arenas is nonetheless profound; it can cause shifts within them, some being serious and problematic. (An example would be a man who is more married to his career than to his wife.)

166

From personal experience, I remember my career as not being my life's centerpiece, for all the other five life arenas clearly were (and are) highly important. But it was the dominator. Most of the other life arenas, in various degrees, were influenced by the broad, day-to-day living parameters, demands, and constraints of career.

To qualify this: Careers certainly aren't evil, but neutral; maybe, in a sense, wonderful is a better term! – food on the table, clothes on the back, work fulfillment, etc. But wonderful doesn't necessarily mean dearly loved. Yet they can be. Career, thusly, is an enigmatic, domineering, steering force during the large multi-decadal chunk of our lives: the working years.

Career—the Benevolent Dictator

The essence of career's power and dominance lies in its obvious universal necessity—that of providing a living. To make a living means we "do what it takes". What it takes, of course, varies depending on type of work, the company's demand structure, and our individual degree of connectivity and commitment to that structure. Indeed, many variables.

Oddly, we tend not to focus on the strong influence career applies to other arenas of life because we're not usually in touch with the invisible undercurrent it applies.

Career is the *infrastructure* of everyday life—the basic, underlying framework; the main director of the breadwinner's daily activity.

Here's career's mysterious penetration: We can slowly become personally defined, both to self and others, by our career identity, not by the more genuine person that may be living somewhere underneath. We can be so wrapped up in career life that our genuine personal identity can be masked to the point even we lose contact with the essential themes of our core being.

There are two important implications of this inner identity shift caused by the weightiness of the career life arena:

1. The *demands* of career can directly influence, often in negative ways, adjacent life arenas that are every bit as

valuable, some even more so. To illustrate, our work indirectly tells us where we will live; i.e., we are usually forced to live geographically close to the centrality of our daily work activity. Career tells us when to rise, what to wear, how to act; it imposes guidelines that, otherwise, would be dictated more on a personal, self basis.

2. The *structure* of career means career strongly affects life's major decision making (Chapter 13), *relieving us of that responsibility.*

Crucial concepts:

• Work is the authority that abdicates our having to *determine* much of our lives for ourselves.
• Career becomes a governor of our lives during the working decades. This outside governorship isn't necessarily a bad thing, but when *retirement* enters the scene, the change of fundamental environment, from career to post-career, renders profound effects that can be problematic, even destructive.

I'm thinking that as you read the above; specifically, what's said about *who* governs our lives, it may strike you adversely, something like, *"What! Are you saying I'm not in control of my own life?"*

There's a distinction to be made here. In many areas of living, each of us does control the way we live. Career, however, is one of those subtle powers of life that can cause invisible, personal lop-sidedness. How so? Career nicely accomplishes two important aspects of life:

1. Maintains relative life security by providing finances, but it also

2. Subtly directs much of our personal direction, keeping much of life activity both in pace, and in place. If you don't believe me, just ask your boss!

Carefully look what's inherent here. With career mostly in charge, *we aren't responsible* for making many of the personal decisions we otherwise would be making. Career is foundationally the director of our days.

For example, the work years cause us to forfeit the duty of making some major life-changing decisions that, were it not for career, we would have to undertake. This shifting of responsibility occurs as many life issues fall under the authority of the career umbrella.

An instance of this occurred in my life a decade or so ago. I had been with a good and prosperous company for probably fifteen years at the time, but wanted to relocate, keeping my position with the company. Understandably, from the company's perspective, the request was denied for justifiable reasons.

My request and desires were valid, but bud-nipped by career. I was (unfortunately) relieved of any need or responsibility of having to seriously plan new life parameters for my family and me, in a new geographic location.

Because such issues are handled by the career apparatus, in some ways, career assumes the unsolicited role of mid-life nanny!

All this changes when retirement arrives.

We then become the ones responsible for major life decisions. But—do we know our true selves well enough so that when the career props are removed, we have necessary inner capacity to be the "infrastructure" of our own lives?

Or, bluntly, is retirement greeted by a scary *vacuum,* centered in ill-preparedness caused largely by unnoticed dependence on the mid-life nanny—career?

Retirement's Missing Link is designed to:

1. Expose subtle deceptions, present caveats, and warn of potential pitfalls of life which can misguide pre-retirees into thinking confidence and assurity reign concerning later years when, in fact, such attributes may be more illusional than actual.

2. Help the reader look inwardly, doing an honest self-assessment, determining genuine personal identity.

3. Help the reader seize that identity, bring it into line with individual life meaning, pursuits, and ambition.

4. Practically apply this new clarity and determination by preparing a plan for as successful retirement, post-career life as possible!

In actuality you, the reader, are a one-person team, a "one-man-band", headed for retirement stardom! I'm your advocate, your coach, your cheerleader. Let's keep going!

WHAT YOU NEED TO KNOW:

- Being true to self is the valid path to know core identity.
- Take a personal inventory to determine how much career has influenced the person you really are.
- Realize that although your career largely steered much of your personal life as well, in retirement you will now be the manager of who you really are and the director of life activities you will pursue. More on this in the next chapter...

Important:

- My most important aspect of retirement consulting and coaching is this: *to help you discover who you really are,* then help guide you in personal objectives most suited to the person that is uniquely—you.

18

Enter—Retirement

It's a Friday. Everybody's said good-bye with well wishes and the retirement party is over. A "job well done" comment from the top helps revitalize the emotional slump not seeing these folks much anymore has brought on.

An engraved watch—that's nice, too. But melancholy worsens, racing through your thoughts. It starts to sink in that, yes, I really *am* this old. I have money, some plans…. "But, but half my life is in *this* place!" You remember the entry interview. Events of the years race through memory at blazing speed. There were good times and bad, but mostly you latch onto the good.

One by one, everybody heads for home; the party had to be after-hours, so already the weekend is chinked. The exodus is quicker than you'd like…. "Are (were) these people *really*, well, friends? At least *some*? Is the weekend *that* important?" You rationalize, "They have private lives and families, too. Maybe I'm just being too sentimental. And, hey. *They* gotta come to work Monday!" Your spirits perk…. You're outta there! For good or for worse, here you go—

(Oh, one other unseen guest was at the party as well. You never got to say goodbye; in fact you never realized he was there. That guest is now gone, too; *for good!* You may see some of your close work associates again, but the 'director'—who helped direct your life all those years—has departed as invisibly as he arrived when your career began.)

The Mid-life Nanny Has Also Retired

It's true. Once the retirement paradigm is entered, that mid-life nanny of all those years, who had been so instrumental in orchestrating life around work, has left the new retiree stark naked in the life planning segment of retirement:

Ready, aim, fire!

—or is it more like—

Aim, (eh) fire?, reddddddy… Are you really—ready?

It's now up to **you,** the retiree, to be the dream-weaver, organizer, captain, the maker of all life's major decisions—'till death when you part, frankly. You are in charge now!

All the old props that defined identity in the career are now gone. This means the personal and emotional support garnered from career influence, both at the job, and by extension at home, has been removed.

That presence wasn't much realized, if at all during the career, but now gone, the absence is in-your-face obvious.

All of a sudden there are no friends at the office; no accolades; no job satisfaction. Although the freedom from duty demands and constraints is a relief, now it's up to you, the newbie director of life, to satisfactorily direct the free time, energies, and direction.

*"Sounds **fine with me!**"* you say, right? Well, yes. Many people heading for retirement tell me that very same thing:

"I can't wait! I've worked long enough; paid my dues in life. Now it's time to really live and do what I want to do!

Well, certainly, after thirty-forty years of the daily grind most everybody *"can't wait"* for a change! I mean, does the sun rise in the morning!? The refreshment reminds me of a hot, humid, summer day, little breeze, with streams of salty sweat running down the face from hoeing weeds in the corn patch, burning the eyes continually. That's a grind! Many a time I can remember that same "can't wait" for some repose and an ice-cold lemonade in the shade!

Pardon my backyard garden sarcasm. I get hyped because I've seen far too many pre-retirees not give one twit about anything in retirement other than "now it's *my* time to live"!

They retire and in a year or two find retirement not what they'd thought it would be, having likely put more effort and planning into family vacations than into a retirement that may last twenty-thirty years! And add to that duration, lack of planning for increased aging and its complications.

Some of my clients are already retired. Their consensus, with my own findings supporting it, is if a retiree hasn't put some effort into planning for life meaning and direction during pre-retirement, once the transition is made and the initial honeymoon period of one to two years is over, the *"fine with me!"* isn't so fine anymore.

The extensive Ameriprise retirement study *The New Mindscape* (Chapter 4) and other gerontological/retirement-based findings fully support this notion.

You can probably tell by now, part of my overarching endeavor is to build a convincing encouragement, urging boomers to begin to take the last part of life seriously.

Not everyone, obviously, acknowledges or agrees. Much of the boomer community is oblivious to sober planning and life purpose development, largely because of societal culture's powerful effort in defining retirement by practically *telling* us to kick back, have fun, make "every day a Saturday", and don't worry about a life purpose. Eat, drink, and take your Viagra, for tomorrow you die." Such makes for a fulfilling, enriching late-term endeavor, do you suppose?

Vacuum

In our retirement context, let's apply the word vacuum. In short, vacuum concerns arriving at retirement not prepared enough to shoulder major life decision making.

A vacuum is a void; a hole. The words *empty space or hollowness* also fit well. Many retirees, once they've really settled into retirement, report hollowness—something's missing. This void becomes prominent during what we know to be the transition part of the career to retirement change (Chapter 16).

An emotional, psychological vacuum can be dangerous.

The laws of physics sometimes apply to emotions as well as to the physical universe. In other words any vacuum begs to be filled. If retirees don't fill that space with something positive and substantial, boredom and worse can easily fill the void. It's *crucial,* therefore, that we learn and plan how to make the filling of that vacuum worthwhile and somehow rewarding. Fortunately, the New Retirement paradigm, in many cases, offers that opportunity.

You don't have to trust my stand on this issue: the data is out there revealing the hollowness. There are simply too many warm, retired bodies who dwell in the retirement vacuum. Sometimes it needs to be witnessed, often which means living with a retiree, in order for masks to come off, exposing unsatisfactory life reality. If you ask retirees what they think of their retirement, usually you get the positive reports. Much of this is straight-forward honesty—we'll take all we can get! But that ugly identity vacuum is far more prevalent than is observed; I see too much of it.

Loss of, or more accurately, in most cases, misplaced identity leads to aimlessness. From there, actually a prison existence is possible—life can be active, but in the mind, the retiree walks in circles; usually very small ones.

Finding a Settledness

You may be thinking, what I've sometimes been reprimanded for doing, especially during the early part of retirement conversations. The dialog goes something like this:

"You make retiring sound so difficult. What's so hard about it? Nobody else is telling me this stuff… I'm really looking forward to having my reward and you're dampening it for me."

Well, retirement can be peachy-pink and not difficult at all, if our focus behind that reviling attitude is limited to society's "just go for it" retirement mentality. But as we know, that's not anywhere near complete reality.

Let me be clear; many retirees *do* go into retirement, contemplating their futures well past the glitz. But not *enough* do. The image of retirement society presents is extremely persuasive, because its message appeals more to self-pleasure than to self discipline, self control, and foresight which, ultimately, are the only true providers of balanced life *confidence and satisfaction*. If these two components lack, can much happiness and joy in later life be expected?

A good word describing reasonable life confidence and satisfaction is *settledness,* which is not a state of superlative life balance, necessarily, but one of an adequate, peaceful existence within—the ability to live with self, others, and our immediate environment. Peace, in our retirement context, is the ability to adjust to a very imperfect world while maintaining good, balanced perspective; enjoying the good and sufficiently dealing with what's not.

Also, *settledness* stems more from joy than happiness. Although both are desirable, joy is more enduring; happiness more fleeting and circumstantial. Happiness tends to come and go, depending on the continual, variable winds of life's events; ever-changing. Joy has more bedrock; it's rooted in a *developed attitude* of the heart, usually having a connection to quality principle, and acquired through the testing of time.

Is Retirement...

- Easy or difficult?
- A time for personal reward and expansion?
- A relatively good time in life, but tainted with deterioration and negative?

Actually, it's a combination of all three:

- *Ease or difficulty?* These terms are relative; one retiree's ease can be another's difficulty. And vice versa.
- *Personal reward and expansion?* You bet! Part II is all about determining your best options in retirement that can lead you to experiencing the term I've often used, *"maximizing later-life."*
- *A relatively good time in life, but tainted with deterioration and negative?* Yes. We are dealt a mixed bag in life and must learn, especially in retirement, to work with what we have.

In stark terms, retirement success or failure has a lot to do with our approach to it and what we, individually, perceive retirement to be. This book is designed to broaden and deepen your later-life perspectives. As perspectives are refined and solidified, you are in good position to best develop your own best plan of approach, however that best fits your individual lifestyle.

Retirement is not about the free time or all the perquisites of post-career living we can garner, or about how troubling aging can be. It's more about learning to determine truth and reality of life, not be swayed by society's "public opinion", *and then going for personal reward and expansion* with all the gusto possible!

Once in a while as I write, I ask myself, "Who do I think I am?" writing all this, wondering why anyone should take me seriously. Well, I'm certainly not one who has, or claims to have, 'right' answers? It goes something like this:

I offer you a fish caught in SEAL: *The Sea of Experience, Age & Learning.* All I know is that the fish is edible. I, and others, have eaten of the variety and, so far, we're all alive and well. So, it's up to you to consider the quality of the catch. Then, if you see fit, simply eat the meat and spit out the bones.

If by the time you've completed this reading you do see wisdom in personal retirement planning, you'll be in *optimal position for systematically determining* personal success, achievement, contentment and peace in your future years of the retirement/renewal phase of life, regardless of the willy-nilly ideas of society in general.

A Conspicuous Absence— What's Missing Here?

Remember that our life course is roughly comprised of thirds:

- life phase one—the formative and educational years
- life phase two—mid-life and career
- life phase three—retirement and old age.

During *"life phase one"*, society puts high premium on getting children and teens well trained for the enormous paradigm shift the young will incur when they enter the work force. From learning to read and write, through high school, and on to maybe college or career-specific training, the early stage of development (life's first third, roughly) is incessantly preparing for the mid-life stage, *"life phase two"*. Well and good!

Our society, like that of most developed countries, has in place a strong preparation agenda for our young; we broadly call it upbringing and education. The *entire society supports and promotes* it all. America not only preps its young in academics but, to a degree, in personal education as well. Our youth get some advance training in integrating with the culture as a whole (social studies and related) and in understanding themselves in relation to it (psychology, spirituality, etc.). All in all, by the time late teen/early twenty years roll around, we have a first phase age group that society, in general, has prepared for the next.

But what about *life phase three,* retirement and old age. What does society have in preparation offing for those in the last of life's phases? Not much. It's all about youth and production.

Production & Youth: the Perfect Marriage

It goes without saying that basic education and training—of *youth*—is rational and crucial for any society or group culture to survive, let alone flourish.

But why are we a throw-away generation, considering retirement and aging?

We've already covered some of the influencing factors in earlier chapters that provide reason for lack of interest in the older crowd. We may touch on a few in review here, but will integrate some important new detail as well.

For the most part, the whole of society is about *production;* human value is often defined by, and tied to, human contribution (producing something), both individually and for society as a whole. This makes sense in many ways, as society is a sum total of people and the level of environment they create, in which they live.

The given—we live; produce; die. Intrinsic to that statement is the obvious:

Youth means activity, productiveness, assertion and advancement.

Aging (by comparison) means relative inactivity, declining productiveness, regression, and deterioration.

Every culture on earth experiences the same contrasts, but not every culture is so wrapped up in youth and self, that aging is considered a hindrance.

Sad Commentary

This brings around again the Pleasure Principle-based mentality. Self likes to be pleased, aggrandized and, because of such proclivity, avoids things and issues—*and people*—that can't contribute positively to the go-get-'em societal mentality.

Especially America and Western Europe suffer the most from this social pathology. Some, if not most cultures of the east, for example, differ greatly by esteeming and regarding their elderly highly. Offspring honor their elders, attending to personal and physical provision, as best possible, till death.

Our elder generation rejection activity (generally unspoken) is particularly sad commentary in current America. It's not to be implied Americans ignore the elder generation. Instead the aging *shadow* is cast, even if outright rejection of the unproductive is masked by "putting up with...."

Much of this usually indirect spurning of the relatively unproductive finds its root in this last generation—the one in which *we boomers grew and now live.* Incriminating isn't it? If you don't agree, please hear me out and see if all this doesn't cohere and make sense by the end of our time together.

In Chapter 7, I described the 'illness' with which many boomers, certainly not all, suffer:

Social Pathology—a $ucce$$ driven, me-first mentality, all too often devoid of the sound Judeo-Christian principle adhered to by our parents' and preceding generations.

[It is mainly *because of* the wisdom of the Founding Fathers that boomers today have had the remarkable opportunity for the success we enjoy. We have truly been the "… land of opportunity…"; *"Only in America"* (Jay & the Americans, 1963). Our "We the people…" constitutionally based individual liberties and freedoms have made the American experience the beckoning "Light on a hill…" to all the oppressed.]

Because of this obsession with youth, self, and things, retirees who aren't actively prosperous and productive are seen to be undesirable (again, unspoken). Enter: older people who aren't generally productive anymore (by street standards), and who don't contribute in much extent to the Gross Domestic Product.

What all this raises in our mover/shaker, youth-oriented culture is a red flag signifying that the over-the-hill gang isn't deserving of a lot of attention. With such slant, retirees are obviously at disadvantage; they are not at all production oriented, progressively need care, can cost their families money, take up space, give off CO_2 destroying the environment!!!—I mean, can ya blame society as a whole for not putting much value on this sort of *liability?*

Although it's not at all right or commendable, it all makes logical rationale to a societal mindset largely infected with self and encumbered with the weight of a non-productive, expensive, time-consuming by-product called the elderly. Heavy.

If you've traveled the northeast and New England, can you remember the many old homesteads (affectionately "old stonies" and farmhouses) that yet endure? Such houses are often found complete with several additions, added progressively through the years. These extended living units not only maintained community within the family, but provided needed care. Children would grow up, have their own, requiring a place to live. Their elderly, likewise, needed accommodation and could find such by adding on to the farmhouse. With the accommodations came a sense of belonging. (Remember—The Waltons?)

I realize valid counter arguments might arise debating that the whole system of life "was different then; we can't compare another way of life to today's". Certainly it was different; no elderly villas, nursing homes, multi-tiered care giving. But also, money wasn't god. And success wasn't measured in dollars to the extent it is today. Speaking of God, He still had a place in public square.

It is not intended here to exalt the social mores of prior eras, or to demean those of our own. Merely to say, in current society and because of the dynamics within it, pre-retirees lack a societal environment that is conducive to deep, qualitative preparation for the third phase of life.

If this isn't corrected, many will retire into an elderly environment that will probably continue in its decrease of regard toward the elderly. Either the environment needs to change or the boomer needs to be prepared to weather what may come.

We won't leave this chapter on a sour note. Now it's time to break out of the toughness of Part I.

Parts II brings genuine retirement optimism. There is a new silver lining to life in later years, one that's never been available to any previous generation! I'm not implying life on a silver platter, certainly, but opportunity. If apprehended by the attentive observer, opportunity can mean the difference between a ho-hum or worse retirement experience and one that, comparatively, glistens.

PART II

Aiming Toward Retirement Fulfillment

**What you need most
to build a successful retirement
is information—
information about *you*!**

19

Defining Today's Retirement

It Ain't Our Daddy's Retirement No More!

If some parents of we boomers are still alive, I wonder what they think of the current retirement panorama compared to that they've known. In some instances, I'm not sure they would recognize a difference, as their points of perspective may be limited—the result of a retirement paradigm so ingrained in their everyday lives. But much *has* changed.

For starters, I wonder if our parents would realize that approximately 10,000 pre-retirees *become retirees, every day* in America. From 2011 on, the ranks will swell at even greater proportion as the official boomer becomes of age: born 1946, retiring 2011—age 65. Crazy numbers, aren't they? It's estimated there are about 70 million baby boomers ready for the charge—an unprecedented, demographic phenomenon that will affect society as a whole for decades to come.

So What's Going On Here…

Boomers are retiring earlier and living longer. That's the bottom line, but not the end of the story. As this occurs, many of us are staring at the likelihood of, let's say as an average, another 25–30 years of life. As developed in Part I, I'm not here to tell you we'll all be hot-rods for those years; quality life can be cut short the day after retirement. But as a rule, if we retire anywhere from, say, 55–65 the chances of many of those years allowing high, personal, productivity are high.

Consider the broad, positive aspects of life the contemporary boomer can enjoy as compared with previous generations of retirees:

- Greater affluence (not necessarily richer, but enjoying a higher standard of living and quality of life than did our parents when they went into retirement)
- Better educated
- Far more technologically advanced
- More free time
- Healthier
- Often retiring earlier (2010 avg.—age 57–58)

Sew these advantages together and we have the makings of having a standard of retirement living that provides opportunities largely foreign to retirees of an earlier day.

The exponential increase in our knowledge base, coupled with more available time means we can stimulate our minds toward broader understandings, even loftier ideas and goals, should we choose—and *not* having to concentrate solely on old age survival!

Retirement today is also much more active and mobile. Our interest breadth has been allowed to widen considerably. The static plop-at-home-rocking chair existence yet exists, if desired, but so much more is available. More time, more knowledge, more advances—all these combine to put the retiree in position to continue to take command of life instead of yielding to the static monotony of the proverbial rocking chair.

Retirement mobility can take different forms:

- If desired, brand new "always wanted to do" careers are possible.
- We can expand our education into areas of real interest.
- Our spiritual personhood can be deepened; volunteerism or church involvement can now be released because of available time.

The real beauty of it all is *we,* not the corporation or organizations, are now the captains of this daily activity. There's that new sign on your life's door: *"Under New Management"*. We are free to roam, explore and then apprehend a lifestyle that *fits* each of us as individuals.

Differences between the Old and New Retirement Paradigms

To put all this into perspective, can you remember your parents *reading books* on retirement? Years ago practically no one wrote much about the whole of the retirement experience. Some emphasis on money organization was usual fare, but little more. The old retirement paradigm usually consisted of collecting a pension, enjoying rest/relaxation, and sensing release from career demands.

Before long, though, and all too often, the rest/relaxation became old. That oldness then began to change emotional outlooks, which then became the order of most daily living, reinforcing the sense of boredom and letdown. Not good. Borrowing from *Change and Transition* (Chapter 16) along this line of thought, the *change*—moving away from career life had taken place causing the *transition*—dealing with the resultant emotional fallout. All this led to a retiree running on a mostly empty gas tank. The quality, upbeat, early retirement attitude and perspective began losing ground, all too often resulting in all manner of negative outcomes.

I can remember my father-in-law looking ahead to his retirement time when there'd be no more work hassles, time schedules, and uncooperative co-workers. He'd thought those pains of work life would abate resulting in an "everyday's a Saturday" existence.

Well, in part that occurred, but he also found he missed old work buddies and the structure of daily life that had actually made career more interesting than he'd thought while actually living it.

During the seventies, he entered retirement living-- smack-dab within the classic old retirement model experience, having no pre-retiree guidance, books, or direction that would emphasize personal retirement planning. In fact, at the time, such things weren't part of retirement thought.

In short he, and so many others, lacked any *vision* for the last third of life. Vision and opportunity simply weren't mainstream retirement vocabulary back then. He lived twenty-five-plus years after retiring and, on occasion during that time, commented to me something to the effect he just didn't "have it" anymore. It was sad.

Dr. Richard Johnson, Ph.D, a noted gerontologist and former president of the American Association for Adult Development and Aging, in his book *The New Retirement*, offers the best assessment criteria I've found for explaining *old and new retirement characteristic comparisons*. I'm indebted to his insight:

> *"For generations, old retirement thinking offered..."*
> (and still does, if perpetuated by today's retirees) *"... a dreamy illusion of prolonged vacation. But for most that result never materialized, offering only shallow satisfaction instead. What was hoped to be rest and relaxation more developed into boredom than the nirvana-like place anticipated."*

He goes on to site specific old and new retirement characteristic comparisons, in one or two word phrases, which are very telling and need to be strongly considered in *your* determination of what you expect retirement life to be.

Dr. Johnson's observations, listed below, are based on practically a lifetime of gerontological, hands-on work and study. His findings confirm and align with those of many others involved in issues of retirement and aging, including my own. The further one studies and analyzes the entire retirement landscape, the more *truthfully obvious* all these comparisons become. As I hold no doctorate in gerontology, I trust if you can't put substantial credence in my observations, that if nothing else—for your very own sake—you do so with those of Dr. Johnson. He's on the mark.

The following isn't quoted verbatim, but presents Dr. Johnson's foundational key points (I'll <u>underline</u> each), concerning the life outcome differences between what the old and new retirement models produce. My observations are interspersed as well.

The new retirement is entirely different from the old. Of course, both involve a withdrawal from pre-retirement life experience, but it's the attitudes and perspectives between each that reveal the most dramatic—and *important*—differences:

- The **old** retirement model produced (and unfortunately still can produce, if adopted by boomer age retirees) a progressively advancing self-forfeiture, powerlessness, and reliance on others. Comparatively,
- The **new** model fosters life enrichment, healthy self-ownership, transformation, and creative self-reliance.

- The **old** model encourages a growing sense of reality denial—a pulling away from what's been known to be real and invigorating, and then leads into an alienation from the original sense of reality;
  - involved also is an increased self-absorption and evolving attitude of criticism, both stemming from the growing dissatisfaction with life in general.
- The **new** retirement model encourages a sense of involvement, not alienation. This originates in an attitude of simply getting past self, the root of many life maladies;
  - promoting healthy self-esteem and physical wellness, for instead of wallowing in attitudes of decline and increasing darkness, the 'new' retiree sees light, instead.

- The **old** model pressures and distorts relationships, probably comprising its chief, overall offense.
- The **new** model enhances relationships because of new interpersonal communication, cohesion, and adaptive freshness.

The old retirement paradigm promotes the illusion of "you've arrived!"—the idea of "everyday's a Saturday. What it actually delivers is sameness and monotony—continually increasing. This being the case, it's easy to understand how interpersonal relationships, especially within family, can be pressured and ultimately deteriorate.

If we use Dr. Johnson's comparative key terms (under-lined above) of old versus new retirement results criteria—and we can because they are statistically and experientially verifiable—*is it not crucial* that the individual boomer understand how these dramatic attitudinal retirement differences play directly into actual approaches to retirement planning?

If the differences between the old and new retirement culture paradigms *are* understood, boomers *can purpose to choose* the benefits of the new, which importantly can negate many of the negative results of the old.

Without being sensitive to the distinction between the two, how can choice for the better be even realized?

The 'Old' Retirement—
Still Available, but Risky

Based on established data and experience of recent decades in gerontological circles, common knowledge has it that remaining with the old retirement life paradigm is risky today for the same reason it was problematic in previous generations. The risk involves the same withering away—seeing life as essentially over, focusing on things that can't be done anymore, perceiving all that's been done to be now lost, being a burden to self and others.

The old retirement model, compared to the new, is as if the candle of life's flame is dimming as opposed to a light-filled, open door. The contrast between the two approaches to retirement is starkly different. As discussed in Part I, in several ways life reality in later years can be a dimming event. Although we can't control advancing time and its sister, aging, *we can control* how we react to their relentless advance in our lives. The key to so doing is to get that concept in motion—starting 'yesterday'.

Favorable Odds

Wish though we might, there's no golden key to the elusive, highly fickle Golden Years of *any* generation, including the Boomer Generation. Nor will there ever be. I don't mean to paint new retirement/later life in pastels of ever-soothing hue. "Life happens!", and with it come challenges and disappointments—ever so common to man....

What is clear, however, is that new opportunity is 'in the air' in a way totally unprecedented. Personal opportunity waits, as the advances of medicine, technology and increased wealth can, and have, allowed.

But it's *up to the individual baby boomer* to apprehend later life's possibilities; go after and seize them! They don't rain down as pennies from heaven. Individual seeking brings forth valuable, personal findings, wrapped in a nice package of quality preparation.

Society as a whole doesn't at all promote, or even observe, fundamental shifts in retirement living. Society is an abstract entity; it obviously can do nothing on its own. Everything depends on the actions of its component parts: you and me.

Good preparation yields good retirement living, at least in those things of life over which we have some control.

Life's too short to go into the last third without a plan that can bring some settledness to the soul.

You, my reader, possess both gusto *and* sober sense in looking to your later life. You must, for you wouldn't have read this far if you didn't.

Go for it!

20

Things Are Different Now

As we've reviewed, many of today's pre-retirees aren't actually aware that a major, dramatic shift in retirement opportunity awaits and is available to them. That's one issue.

The other—just because we have available new retirement options earlier generations didn't, doesn't mean they will be necessarily acted upon. Not all boomers will have the necessary fire and gusto to pursue later life opportunities, declaring instead something like:

> *"Things may be different now, but I'm content to live out my days just coolin' it. Kick back and enjoy life. See what happens."*

This attitude makes initial good sense and is to be respected, but…

Although boomer retirees adopting this 'old' retirement-style perspective will appear to have retirement by the tail, below the surface lays the unseen, very real potential of *living out* the 'old' retirement paradigm. This isn't a particularly good thing.

Do you remember the two key characteristics of the old retirement paradigm? Leisure lifestyle and lack of overall life direction usually led to (and still can) Dr. Johnson's noted issues of increasing self-absorption, passive alienation, and general increasing of withdrawal from others and general reality; i.e., getting stuck in late-life's *self-life* rut—a bad place to be.

Aging and deteriorating health are one thing, but resigning to their mastership, before absolutely necessary, is another.

Most all pre-retirees realize retirement patterns have

changed, but many don't internalize how differentiating between the old and new retirement models can eventually influence retirement life on a daily basis.

Unfortunately, many boomers still view retirement through
their parents' eyes, not recognizing profound shifts have and
are occurring that pose a dramatic shift of retirement adjustment—mostly, in fact, *for the better.*

From a common sense viewpoint, retirement plans made
today *should* be, for the most part, fashioned in a way foreign
to that of our parents' generation. A mere few decades ago,
planning and *retirement* didn't fit well in the same thought pattern—sort of mutually exclusive concepts. The idea then was
more a winding down, a pulling back from the hustle-bustle
known as—work. Pure and simple. Today, the retirement
landscape has changed.

Retirement *basics* do remain the same: save, retire, and enjoy life as best possible. It's the *details* that are profoundly different. This shift means a completely new approach involving:

- a genuine funneling of ambitions
- realizing and embracing opportunity
- adjusting life attitude
- doing more planning involving how time is spent
- application of individual talents and abilities
- dealing with extended aging
- flow of money, and much more.
- You'll note all these pursuits are positive and encouraging.

At core, today's retirement involves a total re-think approach of our parents' retirement experience.

It centers on how we define, think, and feel about our relationship to it, all of which leads us to

Two crucial points of focus:

- The need to grasp the reality that retirement is truly the
  mother of all life's changes and transitions. This perception of retirement was unknown by earlier generations,
  and is unrecognized by most boomers today.

- Realize such complexity creates the *work* of making some life choices, convictions, and decisions ahead of time. Sounds like a great effort is involved, doesn't it... "Who *needs* it!" you might think. Well, let's put it into perspective.

Although we now live longer, deal with more complexity, and have some pre-retirement organization to do, we *have planning resources from which to draw, and gerontological data sources* to warn of the pitfalls *if we don't.* Virtually none of this existed during the previous generation's pre-retirement years.

All of a sudden the work load of taking retirement seriously doesn't seem so laborious. Consider all the good:

- To be able to plan ahead with optimism
- To be living in a time of life which actually offers an unfolding of new challenges, discoveries, and options.

Doesn't all this sound better than the old sense of gradual withering away due to an ill-perceived sense of increasing worthlessness?

Note: a plug here for the RSP (Retirement Success Profile) might be appropriate. The RSP 'pulls together' a boomer's thoughts, desires, and life omissions that center around forming the whole of their retirement vision. More to follow on the RSP.

Gerontology—It's a Good Thing

Keep in mind advances in medicine, education, and technology are allowing today's retiree to usually retire earlier, live healthier longer, and enjoy a higher standard of living than generally did our parents. To support this, let's quickly review *gerontology*—the study of social, psychological, and biological aspects of, and impact on, aging.

Gerontologists didn't even exist prior to World Wall II, so our parents had absolutely no benchmark source of reference, heading into life's last *developmental phase*—retirement. Today, just the fact that books like this are being written as general retirement guides is a direct result of available gerontological understanding. More than an entire generation of developing gerontology now helps us—ahead of time—be aware of needed later life forward direction, warning signs, and pitfalls, all of which earlier generations just had to meet head-on when encountered.

Throughout the book I've repeatedly use the term *developmental phase* when referring to retirement. Imagine! Can you see your parents, say, back in the sixties, actually perceiving retirement to be a time of personal *development?* Yes and no, I suppose, depending on the individual, but essentially retirement wasn't about life *developmental* opportunity—a time to expand personal horizons and foster life fulfillment and enrichment!

Instead, all previous generations had no inkling whatsoever that retirement could be a time of kick-starting life to a new level—because at that point on the American societal development timeline, it simply wasn't. Physically and philosophically, retirement then wasn't oozing optimism! Instead (as we've discussed) it was seen as exactly the opposite—a time of gradual withering away, cloaked in reasonably attractive garb of keeping busy and not having to work anymore. As well, life expectancy, even as close as the last generation, was seen to be shorter than what's perceived, and actually is, today.

Seize the Day!

Previously I'd used the phrase, "Under New Management", a term describing the state of affairs in which a retiree has cut the cord of the corporate, multi-decadal 'nanny', and finds him/herself now completely in charge of managing everyday life.

That's *you*—soon to be!

When you retire all the props, of what amounted to your career directing much daily life activity, disappeared. Once retired *you,* not the old career's influence, are now in charge of charting your own course for the rest of *your* life.

Let me qualify and clarify here: I'm *not* saying

- you are to be a Marine sergeant unto yourself, developing some sort of unusual, odd-ball, retirement discipline
- nor that retirement means the same thing to all retirees—no, no, no…
  - For some, retirement goals and pursuits have nothing to do with personal growth and fulfillment at all, even though today's retirement environment makes provision for it. Some retirees find simply maintaining the leisure mentality is precisely the "charting" of the rest of their lives that suits them best. Fine and good.
  - At the other end of the spectrum, some retirees have ambition to actually start new careers, something they've always "wanted to do" (like me, writing, starting my own consulting business and attempting to help others of my generation).
  - There are many who desire retirement to center on new educational opportunities, travel, moving near children, volunteerism—something often linked to enhanced spiritual development—and a host of other retirement pursuits too numerous to mention here.

Retirement life can be as varied as colors and arrangements in a kaleidoscope. And all are valid! Truly, "To each his own".

There is a caution, however, concerning anything-goes, purposelessness retirement mentality that has no 'charting' basis to it. Although we acknowledge all retirement styles, planned or not, aren't necessarily right or wrong, if we don't purpose to strive away from the backdrop of what we now know the mainstays of the old retirement paradigm to be, *we risk* what much of the old too often produced—that tendency to pull away from life reality and head toward an ugly, increasing sense of worthlessness.

So—*what **is** it* you need to do to be sure you're heading the right way?

- First, commit to living up to the new sign on your life's door—"Under New Management", understanding you *are* responsible for a retirement game-plan that fits the real you.
- Next, determine—beyond question—your real identity, remembering it may easily have become blurred, even emotionally out of touch, obscured by decades of demanding career and mid-life activity. You only have one chance, really, to get it right; you are heading into life's last developmental phase but *one time*. Be certain you are in touch with yourself as you head there.
- When you know you have reasonably connected with your dreams, passions and pursuits that may have been suppressed for years, you are in position to take positive steps of developmental retirement planning that fits, solitarily—*you*. (Keep in mind the inherent value of taking the Retirement Success Profile with follow-up analysis and consultation.)

Interestingly, not everyone needs some nudging toward reclaiming self's actual identity. Some folks know exactly where they are headed; in fact, maybe have had a charted course during the most or entire time of their lives. Most, however, do not.

My daughter, in her thirties, and at least to this point in her life, is like that. She claims that in her early high school years she had direction that a career related to Art or Interior Design was a clear goal. She set her mind to direction, and today owns a thriving, professional design business. My sons and I, on the other hand, have had to rummage around in life for a while in attempt to secure real direction.

Genes? Life circumstances? God's will? I'm last to presume on such life determinations, but do know this—

All boomers do well to gain grip on personal identity, even if as late as the pre-retirement time of life. How?

- By creating an introspective, retirement roadmap, leading to the real 'you'. (RSP)
- By diligently seeking development of inner preparedness that will lead to strength and resilience for times when life will inevitably make difficult detours from that planned roadmap.

Summarizing:
- Recognize that withering into the 'old' retirement methodology is *not* a sensible option
- Gain hold of personal identity
- *Align* goals, passions, desires and personal convictions with that identity
- Establish retirement goals of quality and virtue that can only feed goodness to your inner person and to others
- Recognize life won't go exactly as planned
- When difficulty comes, rely on your sturdy framework of acquired resilience root—that you've wisely taken the time to build, in a younger day—Don't wait.

Looking Inside—Where We Go from Here

So, just how *do* we get all this "Under New Management" direction in motion?

First, we need to return to those six Life Arenas mentioned earlier: Career; Family; Relationships; Self; Spirit; Leisure. All of daily life, throughout our entire lives, operates within one or more of these spheres. Because this is where each of us lives all of life, these arenas

1. provide a perfect functional structure for

2. formulating a personal retirement life plan.

At this point, I begin to introduce a personal retirement planning system, probably the finest available. It is a creation of Dr. Richard Johnson, Ph.D., the noted gerontologist mentioned earlier. Over the years, he has put together what is called the previously mentioned Retirement Success Profile (RSP), and a subsequent Retirement Options (RO) program, both of which I'm trained and certified to administer. In fact, the excellence of both tools is so considerable, they form the foundation of much of my retirement consulting work:

> *One may know how to build a house, but without appropriate tools, labors in vain in attempt to so do.*

Both retirement tools: RSP and RO have been used effectively for years, internationally, which speaks to their credibility. These tools work.

Neither the RSP or the RO program, however, are part of this book, as the detail of each demands one-on-one consulting interaction between myself and clients. I'll explain more later, should you have interest to delve deeper.

Remembering Our Main Intent

As stressed in **Part I**, the overall intent is *to bring into boomer consciousness an **awareness*** that credible, personal retirement information *is* available to boomers—information that mainstream society doesn't appear to even know exists. Part I gets us past the usual societal retirement focus centered on the public sector's mainstays of finance and leisure.

Part II contrasts the old and the new retirement models. Understanding there *is* a distinct difference between the old and new retirement paradigms enables the boomer to assess real opportunity; opportunity well past that which was available a mere generation ago.

Here in Part II we begin to develop individual life arena *connection* to retirement, equipping you with a basic enablement of beginning to chart your own retirement course. You will get an idea how to begin planning your personal "Under New Management" agenda—all of which is in your control.

You can go as little or far as you wish.

NOTE:

My following information on the six Life Arenas—the NEXT SIX CHAPTERS—is limited to *generalities* about each arena. Reason: every person relates to each arena differently—there's no way to cover such infinite possibilities within a book's context.

Ideally, therefore, absorb each chapter's content, which gives you perspective about each life arena as related to retirement. Then, if possible, immerse yourself in the RSP (Retirement Success Profile) which will maximize your own personal connection to all arenas. It is from the RSP that you, with my help, truly determine your strengths and weaknesses within each life arena, as well as determining which arenas of life are especially important to you. In short—the RSP helps you find 'you'—not the 'you' of career past, but of retirement future!

As we develop each Life Arena, attempt to place yourself into the basic context of what each arena explains. I'll attempt to draw you into each arena, connecting its generality to retirement.

We'll begin in the next chapter with discussion centered on Life Arena #1—Career.

21

Life Arena #1—Career

The Career Life Arena, in our context of its linkage to retirement, is the central life arena. Career profoundly affects what retirement will be. As discussed in Chapter 16, change and transition is all about the migration from our life-long work to life's brand new developmental phase. Much of what we learned and experienced during the career decades directly affects decisions—some good, some not—we make concerning advancing into the retirement period.

The Career arena has to do with everything you connect to your primary work of life: 1) preparation for it, 2) what you do while in it (work!), 3) what you think about in relation to it, 4) even how you will ultimately rest from it (in this thing we call retirement).

CAREER—AS APPLIED TO RETIREMENT:

The Career Life arena involves a letting go of one thing to seize something else. As we change and transition from career to retirement, some functions and associations with career must be released.

Generally, those who have been more personally involved in their careers have most difficulty with the change. We've already talked about identity—here's where it really comes home to roost. Careers have a tendency to not only define what we *do,* but to shape who we *think* we are. Leaving career and going into retirement, therefore, can result in identity turbulence. If retirees can't release former identity definition, there's strong tendency to lose quality retirement traction, receding into life indifference, withdrawal, and depression, all of which express an emotional and psychological decay.

Career—What to do:

As a pre-retiree, *now's* the time to think deeply about your emotional connection to your career. The Retirement Success Profile (RSP) is the best means of analyzing, in depth, where you currently stand concerning self-identity.

From there, you can make a best determination how to, literally, protect yourself—from yourself. Don't take that as an indictment or insult: we all have to unravel who we really are. Emotional transitioning into retirement is far more complex than meets the eye.

This personal identity topic is so *impactful upon retirement success* that, *if for no other reason,* I'd suggest taking the RSP.

You'll need to be thinking about how to fill the emotional void career loss leaves behind. This involves much more than just "keeping busy & having fun"—society's answer to the issue.

Career—Post-career Options:

Once the identity issues are addressed, you'll be in better position of knowing how to manage those dreams, passions, and desires to which we've alluded in earlier chapters. This retirement management may lead you into considering a variety of retirement options that, to this point, haven't seemed relevant. New ideas can blossom into new life directions—"*I never **thought** of that...!*" That's the point of all this *introspection*: getting to understanding the *you* with whom you may actually not be familiar.

Most later mid-lifers (fifties) find themselves in what might be reminiscent of Rod Serling's The Twilight Zone: We know career is nearly behind us, but just as real as the past has been, retirement is at least as realistic, awaiting with a mix of anxious anticipation and precautionary, healthy hesitation: And which is the reality? We've lived in career; we know we now will live in retirement. Which is the illusion; which is real? We know from where we've come, but exactly *where is it* we are going!?

The idea here is get the anticipation and hesitation well sorted. The only way that's possible is to, as fully as possible, come to a sense of *genuine* identity.

It bears repeating: Genuine, self-realization is really the only satisfactory way of producing a serious base concerning what best individual choices for retirement life may be.

Getting to know genuine identity also takes us to a deeper level—one of self-determination. This means determining to internalize that the past behind us, and the aging before us, are not the determinants of retirement success. We need to learn to make preoccupation with youthfulness and the hatred of physical deterioration subservient to the element of maturation—something we can control:

Maturation is not the equivalent of physical aging!

Maturation has to do with intangibles aging can't influence. If we allow ourselves to be more pre-occupied with the withering physical frame than with the vibrancy of maturation, we close the door to all a mature mind can put to good use.

We need to choose from *two focus options:*

1. *Go the way of society:* Retirement means getting old, unattractive, and unproductive (by business standards). Head this way, and allow the physical to dampen and devalue retirement as a whole.

   -or-

2. Choose the reality that *maturation overrides physical aging:* It's in exercising the genuine, mature self that leads to a multitude of internal, intangible growth areas that can sprout into all sorts of good and virtue.

The New Retirement paradigm allows for internal growth that can be expressed in ways that benefit us and others as well. We, however, have to *choose* to chart that personal course of self-enrichment available to us:

- Choose *life*! Come to really value all the internal growth potential today's retirement allows

    -or-

- wither…according to societal perception of post-career life based on aging's physical deterioration.

If we choose retirement *life*, what might post-career option choices be? In effect, these choices can be as wide as the world is large! The key is getting to the point where the pre-retiree is <u>aware</u> of personal options. The RSP (Retirement Success Profile) is invaluable in unwrapping personal opportunity that well fits the individual's retirement design.

Five Career Considerations

Pertaining directly to the "Career Arena", Dr. Johnson points out an important consideration.

There are five benefits/needs (meaning needs met by everyday career living) that do not go away simply because we retire; they have become a part of us to such a degree that we cannot simply discard them without some emotional, psychological, and even spiritual consequences.

What are the needs/career benefits our careers develop for us which we must somehow replace during our everyday retirement living?

Dr. Johnson specifically considers five, upon which I'll elaborate below. There are probably more. Dr. Johnson's list, however, is over-arching and well suits our purposes here:

1. *Financial Remuneration*—the obvious, of course, but what's interesting is that far too many boomers view *only this* career benefit as the main factor in reproducing success in retirement. In other words, *"I made enough money to be happy during the work years, so if I have enough money for retirement, I'm all set."*

    Here's the dilemma: Such single-focus eliminates the four other needs that must also be satisfied in retirement. If money—and what it can buy (usually leisure)—is the sole work replacement met during retirement, the other four needs will suffer. And so will the retiree!

2. *Time Management*—Do you remember the "props" I mentioned that career provides, and that once career is gone, those props are removed; that is to say, the career 'nanny' has retired as well? My "Under New Management" theme parallels the same idea. In short, once in retirement it will be necessary to fill that void of managing time for which the career had, earlier on, been responsible.

3. *Utility*—A good way to understand utility is the development of sense of purpose. Career has always been a good vehicle that instills a reason to get up in the morning (whether we want to or not!). Career also provides some sense of qualitative satisfaction (whether we like the job or not!). Although most people appear to not particularly favor the work they do, most do sense at least a minimal degree of accomplishment within it.

4. *Status* (Dr. Johnson's term. I prefer *Societal Role*)— during our career life, our lives are given definition by what we do. Regardless of society's perceived level of "status" attained, each of us develops a combined sense of personal worth and identity, measured by our perception of self in relation to our work role. This establishes our role in society.

Interesting: A broom-pusher and a CEO both attain a certain level of status or societal role. Though the level of status is obviously broadly different in this example, consider if *neither* the broom-pusher *nor* the CEO had any job whatsoever. If that were so, neither individual could gain any sense of worth or identity from careers, regardless of societal level.

Something in life has to provide stimulus for personal identity. Work, regardless of its nature or perceived status, is what we humans possess as much of the focal point of such stimulus.

Paradoxically interesting: We have a two-edged sword here. As identity during our work life is mostly created by the career, when we enter retirement—to a degree—that very identity must then be viewed circumspectly and with caution, because the career-created identity is very likely *not* the genuine identity of the authentic self—who we really are at core:

The authentic self is the *truest* essence of who we can know ourselves to be, getting beyond ego, self-esteem, and self-regard. It's *who* we were in our rawest sense, if you will—likely reflecting back to a time our authenticity spoke directly to those hopes, dreams, passions and intended goals. But then...

Career intervened. Meeting the responsibilities of life through our work brought about an unintended shift in personal identity. This is not to say such shifts are good or bad, but if our authentic self has been altered due to career life, in order to be all we can during our retirement, we must revert back to recognizing our authenticity.

The New Retirement model offers a lot of opportunity to express that authenticity. To maximize it all, we must begin with no façades, no self-deception, no put on. If we wear all that junk, we can't have the peace with self otherwise so attainable if we recognize ourselves squarely as the real-deal.

5. *Socialization*—The fifth of Dr. Johnson's work benefits has to do with community: the expression of our career's personal interaction on various levels. Because we spend so much time with the work crowd—more than with our spouses, usually—a developed system of on-the-job personal integration can't help but develop. Held in good check and balance, this community is a personally supportive benefit of working. Work partners, friends, buddies often form deep relationships. Then...Enter retirement—"Where did all that go?!"

Once retirement is underway, winds have changed. It's at that point the retiree needs to have in place some sort of replacement criteria which fills the mostly emotional void career abandonment has initiated.

Summary: Career Life Arena

The Career Life Arena makes a dramatic shift when retirement overshadows decades of work activity. Fortunately, the New Retirement model offers so much more continued life positivism, as compared with the old, that if boomers awaken to the fullness of life that is available to be perpetuated, the retirement future can take on a golden luster.

Choose *life* over withering life decay! Post-career opportunity *coupled with* maturity forms a fabulous combination—we possess a gold mine suitable for Golden Years! Think of that!

22

Life Arena #2—Family

"The Love Chapter"

Career should always be secondary in importance to family. I haven't spoken with Dr. Johnson on why he's placed family as second in his lineup of life arenas; in fact, I don't know that he had any particular order of the six in mind as he finalized on them, other than to say career is number one because it's so integral to retirement. One might conclude career and family are two sides of the same coin.

Nevertheless, retirement can intensify family relationships, especially within marriage. We leave our careers, but family remains.

The family arena includes all interactions with primary and secondary (extended) family members, and strongly involves degrees of satisfaction, intimacy, connectedness, love, and sense of inter-relational well-being.

Specifically, Dr. Johnson points out, and I quote

All other things being equal, a healthy relationship (meaning family relationship) makes for a healthy retirement; an 'OK' relationship makes for an 'OK' retirement; while a chronically sick relationship makes for a disaster.

Usually, family relationship centrally focuses mainly on the husband/wife connection.

We've already established the importance of knowing our

true, personal identity to be probably the most significant life-essential going into retirement. Because family is all about relationship, if we have our own identity and honest self-evaluation in order, how wonderful it can be to integrate that confidence, on a continual basis, within the context of our closest of relationships.

If we can have this relational quality well established with the closest of relationships—where unfortunately it can sometimes be the most difficult to maintain—that sets the stage for a filtering down through the various levels of lesser relationships all the way to, say, a store clerk and distant acquaintances.

Fact of the matter is this: *get it right within;* let that overflow into the closest of relationships; then find it relatively easy to share the same personal attributes with all we meet.

Family—*As applied to retirement*

Once retirement is in place and hubby is taking up space in a domain formerly more singly inhabited, conditions of a healthy relationship are paramount! Retirement changes many things, and one glaring change often centers around husband and wife occupying the same physical space in the home on a much increased frequency. I've had several pre-retirees tell me their spouses at home "can't wait" for them to retire! As well, several retirees and/or their spouses have changed the "can't wait" to "can't stand" once the additional 98.6°F spends too much time in the kitchen!

Dr. Johnson suggests several life arena components within the context of immediate family relationships, two of which I especially believe form the foundation for success within the spousal relationship: **mutuality and respect**. Fundamentally, more marriages fail when these inter-relational factors aren't functioning as they should than for any other reason. If boomers can go into retirement with these essentials in order, almost all other factors, including having enough money, good health, time to 'play' and all the rest, are secondary.

The Truth About Love

Marital mutuality and respect are two direct descendants of the *overarching* rule of love.

How does love *overarch*? It does so by being what we could say is being in highest position of authority. For example, a company's CEO *overarches* authority over all other company employees and what they do. All are subject to that authority.

Genuine love, by definition, is all powerful while, at the same time, is the epitome of humility, never seeking its own. In other words, the authority of love is completely ruling, yet self-sacrificing. Probably the greatest of all paradoxes! Love is the all-in-all authority, but can only manifest itself *if it gives itself away*!

If it remains to itself, say, like a kernel of corn, love remains alone. In fact, we could say it negates itself; it's worth virtually nothing. But if it is planted and dies unto itself, so to speak, it produces nearly incalculable yield!

Along these same lines, I'm reminded of a poem I learned probably forty-plus years ago; so simple, yet significant in explaining love and humility. I don't even know the title, but its words come back to me often:

> *A candle is a lovely thing*
> *It makes no noise at all.*
> *But slowly gives itself away*
> *While quite unselfish*
> *It grows small.*

As does the candle, if love (in general, but particularly in marriage) yields itself for the sake of another, can marital mutuality and respect not be the by-product?

The candle *also* has power to literally destroy; fire is all-consuming! (Talk about authority!) But instead, it "seeks not its own", but offers the gift of light, *yielding* for the *benefit* of others.

When husband and wife reciprocally exchange mutuality and respect with one another, they exemplify the wonder of the candle's *light*, squelching what otherwise would be the presence of relative darkness.

How are mutuality and respect so enabled by the power of love? Because "Love covers (overlooks) a multitude of sin" (in our context, sin means the faults and misgivings of others that directly and negatively affect us personally).

This *covering over,* or looking the other way—when retaliation might well be the alternative emotion—is the crux of meaning for the phrase many of us know as "unconditional love".

Unconditional love is applicable to every facet of life, in one form or another. It is the literal purity of Light in what can be a dark world. The Old Retirement regimen, remember? There was, and is, a lot of darkness in that line of thinking. We need light to saturate the New Retirement!

Marriage, within the retirement context, needs as much, maybe more, emphasis on laying down one's desires for the sake of another than at any other time: It's 'just we two' now. There are no props of kids, career, or other diversions causing reason not to have our mates in the crosshairs of love's true affection.

Married retirees have two options for achieving marital happiness:

1. love with an intentional commitment, of mind and will, to benefit the other, *even if* at self's expense (unconditional love)

   or

2. rely on life's circumstances and fickle feelings of the heart that shift as sand in the sea.

One brings relative stability in a certainly unstable world; the other, risky exposure to the winds of adversity, certain to occur.

Don Francisco, perceptive song-writer said it best: *"Love is not a feeling; it's an act of your will".* Although love is full of feelings, in the sense of truly caring for another, a determination to lay down one's own desires or direction for the sake of the beloved, often at self's expense, is required. This means something to the effect, *"Although I don't find you perfectly lovable, I commit my will to love you, regardless."*

The Perfect Retirement Combo: Love, Mutuality, Respect

A few paragraphs below, you'll notice how genuine love is broadly, but actually, to be expressed on a daily basis: *love's expression in action.*

First, I realize most of us have a general idea of what mutuality and respect are, but want to bring in a key distinction Dr. Johnson uses, in his Family Arena structure, to describe the two terms.

1. **Mutuality**—Dr. Johnson makes an important distinction between what he calls **inter-dependence** and **mutual independence**. It's vital to grasp the difference, as one leads to good outcomes, the other not:

Mutuality is very similar to inter-dependence. Such attitudes form the recognition that each spouse can depend on the other for most all aspects of the relationship;

Mutual independence, on the other hand (a feel-good buzz phrase of contemporary culture), directly opposes counting on one another. It's a cover for "doing my own thing".

In conversation with many pre-retirees I find the attitude, "I pretty much do *my thing*; she does hers—it makes for a good marriage."

Such mutually agreed independence is excellent for good co-habitation, but not for emotional, substantive intimacy within what's traditionally been the secret of marital success. *My thing/your thing* is inherently self oriented. Self, when expressed as serving self, has virtually no room in an other-oriented relationship—what we know marriage should be. To substantiate…

Consider—*(love's expression in action)* the wedding ceremonies you have attended whose center theme revolves around what many know to be "The Love Chapter" of the New Testament—I Corinthians, Chapter 13:

[4]Love is patient, love is kind. It does not envy, it does not boast, it is not proud. [5]It is not rude, it is not self-seeking, it is not easily angered, it keeps no record of wrongs.

⁶Love does not delight in evil but rejoices with the truth. ⁷It always protects, always trusts, always hopes, always perseveres. ⁸Love never fails.

Even those who hold no particular affinity for Scripture would agree the description of real love found there is incomparable; how can it be faulted? It simply bears truthful witness to our inner sensibilities. It's the *real deal*. A saying I'd learned long ago well summarizes "The Love Chapter": *Love always manifests itself in sacrifice toward the object of its affection.*

Me-centered never works! If a man (or woman) retires and is ready to spend lots of time in close company with a spouse, acquiring a position of thinking of her in terms of her welfare and happiness—at his own expense—is crucial. It's the core of Dr. Johnson's term, *inter-dependence*:

Inter-dependence really means *both* partners must assume an attitude of *laying down their own priorities for the sake of the other.*

That popular comment (mentioned above) I often hear from within marriages, *"I pretty much do my thing; she does hers—it makes for a good marriage"*, misses the point of successfully, deep marriage relationship. To a limited point, individual interests and pursuits are certainly valid and should be encouraged and entered into by each spouse. But marital 'cohabitation' is not a good recipe for marital success, long-term. Many people won't come right out and say their marriage operates on such principle, but that's what all too often is occurring within today's marital partnerships.

Caution: Let's say you've been married for decades, and you've been in a career for that same time—a likely scenario. Spending mainly only evenings at home with your wife all that time was one thing: Living at home now 24 x 7 is another. Get the picture?

Can you see the importance of *truthfully* assessing, *during pre-retirement,* where your marriage relationship genuinely stands? If it's not on solid relational ground prior to retirement, and you intend to plop yourself in her presence day-in/ day-out, *some changes in approach to your later years are in order!*

Either putting off retirement or rationalizing, "it will be

fine; we'll *make* it work", aren't anywhere near ideal approaches, especially if you are getting ready to pull the career plug.

Far better, don't you think, would be to deeply consider the relationship's potential for improvement! If you know or suspect you are responsible for most of any obvious marital trouble, why not work on getting right what you've screwed-up all those years. (Now don't get mad at me....) That could mean as little as soul-searching, owning-up to the error of your ways, and committing to change. It could also mean your less-than-desirable ways are so patterned from years of repetition that outside counsel would be beneficial, if not crucial. (I can either provide counsel or recommend outside, certified marriage counseling. I am not a certified marriage counselor, but can offer private counsel that may be helpful.)

Alright. Above I address you, personally, and want you to know I do so with respectful intent. I assume mostly men read this book, and therefore address the husband. Needless to say, all this is applicable to wives as well.

This isn't the place to get further into the aspects of marital help. Suffice to say, whether you are a husband or wife, if you are aware your marriage isn't what it should be:

Please—*strongly* consider how retirement will impact and intensify that relationship.

Attempting to fix what's broken is far better than holding off retirement for fear of deeper marital difficulties:

Could it possibly be that pending retirement is the catalyst that can spur your marriage into getting the attention it's needed for many years? (Tell you what; it did in my case....)

Lastly, while on this sensitive topic, please remember the emphasis on truth. Shakespeare: To thine own self be true. Search your soul, will you? And I share this with you, personally—

As I approached my retirement, I knew—beyond question—I needed help in repairing aspects of marital goodness that over the years I'd *screwed-up* royally. It was time to be ultra-truthful with myself; time to put into practice what I preach! Often times counselors—themselves—need objective perspective; I did. And I sought it out. It's made all the difference.

So, why is truth so important? Without it, we gloss over life's difficulties and unpleasantries, living in sort of a self-deception (deception is another word for lie), choosing to remain in the cozy place where things don't need to be encountered. To re-use an earlier analogy, at our own peril, we often treat our marriage difficulties (any of life difficulties, for that matter) like the toothpaste ad of years ago proclaimed: *Ignore your teeth and they'll go away.* They *don't* go away, they worsen. Decay is decay is decay—whether it's an issue of teeth care or caring for one of the most sacred bonds in life—our marriages.

Let's now move on to the second family life-related component, highly important within the retirement scheme:

2. **Respect**—appreciating, holding sacred and guarded, the uniqueness of one's partner. In a real sense, honor is involved.

Respect is that spin-off of love. Keep in mind the saying: *Love always manifests itself in sacrifice toward the object of its affection.* *Sacrifice* means to place the other person—the object of affection—on a higher plane than our own. *Respect* has a lot to do with that principle. Sometimes the other person may not even deserve respect, but the principle of love and sacrifice allow respect and honor of the other to prevail.

Respecting our spouse doesn't mean either the husband or the wife is a doormat. Rather, it means *even if* a spouse doesn't glisten with perfection or necessarily please our wishes, we hold them in special regard, simply because of who they are: in this case, an extremely close partner.

To illustrate, let's say you're retired and want to hang around the kitchen because you're hungry. Your wife wants some solitude so she can think more clearly about the meal she's preparing to fill your stomach.

Now think back to your career. You didn't show up until supper time; now it's only 4PM and you and she are occupying the same floor space. This is a perfect time to *sacrifice* your desire for food, *respecting* her need for personal space, and *not* holding resentment against her for telling you to scoot! Resentment is the opposite of respect.

Wonderful are mutuality, respect, sacrifice, honor—all some of the finest fruit of love! Even more wonderful is the good that is the outcome! In such circumstances house and home are a heavenly haven, not a headache from hell.

We all do well to anticipate and, if necessary, to prepare for the essential retirement need of marital mutuality and respect, rooted in love.

Care Giving—Determining the Balance

As the decade unfolds, and into the next, seeking a balance that will both provide care to elderly parents (or grown children), but not wreak total havoc in the mind and heart of the care giver, will be increasingly more difficult. There's complete substantiation for all this beginning with the fact that about 75% of all retirees are faced with the added life burden of caring for the elderly. That percentage is almost certain to increase in the coming years.

In Chapters 14 and 15, we examined the implications longer life spans have created. Because medical 'miracles' now extend life, more care giving will be required, both quantitatively and in extended duration.

How much is one to do? Time and again, I encounter distraught, loving boomers who are torn between having to care for an elderly parent(s), remain in a career to provide a living, and view retirement, at least early retirement, with a tarnished optimism—if that.

In attempt to work toward a balanced approach to this ever-growing issue, Dr. Johnson offers several what he calls "... *ingredients which together inject care giving with psycho-spiritual dynamism rather than emotional pain.*"

What he is suggesting, from an obviously gerontological standpoint, is that if caregivers apply "ingredients" criteria, care giving can become personally more uplifting than draining, benefiting both care giver and the care recipient. To quote:

Retirees, and all care givers for that matter, require six "ingredients" which together inject care giving with psycho-spiritual dynamism rather than emotional pain.

Caregivers need to:

1. *Gain understanding into the needs of elders as well as their own.*

2. *Develop truly healthy relationships with their aging parents.*

3. *Know how to break down barriers that may exist between them and their aging parents.*

4. *Foster positive communication between themselves and their aging parents.*

5. *Allow the healing message of their own spirituality to become the core of their relationship.*

6. *Remember that death and mourning are the final end of the care giving process when dealing with aging parents.*

When properly incorporated into the care giving situation, these six principles have the power to transform what might otherwise become a travail of uncertainty and frustration, into a time of personal development unparalleled in one's previous life stages.

What's being implied here is that as the aging dilemma increases, more intimate soul-searching, on behalf of the retiree/care-giver, will be required if the retiree's life balance is to be attained.

Much of this is about knowing where to establish care giving boundaries that are clear to both care giver and recipient. As well, there are two schools of thought involved here; one centering on the Old Retirement model and one on the new: The old paradigm focuses on the idea that retirees are to provide all the care for aging parents; the new suggests retirees become more care *managers* than care givers, procuring outside help where possible.

Dependents

The care giving/dependency issue isn't at all limited to aging parents. Along with the deterioration of traditional marriage has come the increased incidence of multi-tiered families resulting largely from 50%+ rates of divorce and remarriage. This collection of 'relatives' increases the retiree's turmoil and probability of someone within the 'family' needing care in some capacity.

As a whole, retiree care giving deals with a love driven, felt responsibility, heart-rending quagmire. Where the lines are to be drawn has to ultimately be a retiree's personal decision based on circumstances particular to each and every instance.

Addressing this issue well before it occurs, as with all other retirement planning and preparation, is to the boomer's advantage. If your family situation is one signaling care giving of some sort is likely, discussion, strategizing, and at least laying some basic game plan is prudent. Have something in mind ahead of time.

Summary: Family Life Arena

Above, I've briefly centered on what I believe are the *most important sections of the Family Life Arena*—mainly the husband/wife relationship, then care giving and dealing with dependents.

There is much more to be considered regarding the Family Life Arena in relation to retirement. To mention only a few:

- Intimate strengths of marriage
- Intimacy development
- Communication enhancement
- Shared fun
- Money and lifestyle management

Due to limited print space and to try to keep this reading limited to a retirement overview, however, the other family related components are better addressed in the full Retirement Options program, which is outside the parameters of this writing. The Retirement Success Profile (RSP), coupled with the much more complete Retirement Options program will be more fully described in a chapter to follow, should you have interest.

Next, we'll look at the third of the six Life Arenas—Relationships (outside family).

23

Life Arena #3—
Relationships

Although relationships extending past family may or may not be as important, they contribute greatly toward life's core meaning. Life's core meaning has a lot to do with personal contentment and happiness, so the quality of our relationships can impact us directly.

Retirement is a time to maximize the value and experience of relating to others outside the family connection. During career years, there can often be more relational activity than we want, as life demands force them upon us. Of course, during career life we tend to maintain certain especially valuable, personal connections as much as is possible, but the flurry of daily life can easily diminish even those.

Retirement poses a different scenario, affording the luxury of more time for relational prioritization. In other words, we can now choose relationships that tend to increase life's fulfillment. Further, retirement is also the time to appreciate, in depth, the remaining high-value personal relationships that remain! Time does have a way of thinning out the ranks....

The New Retirement paradigm plays into all this nicely. Retiring earlier, generally healthier, and more affluent than the old model provided, we have opportunity to sincerely involve ourselves with facets of life that provide meaningful life gratification, offering what wasn't nearly as perceived, or indeed opportune, in the Old Retirement model.

Some relational opportunities, past the more personal, might include

- church/synagogue
- athletic or other competitive teams
- social contact organizations
- clubs
- community projects.

In other words, whatever you do in your retirement living that provides a balanced sense of acquiring and maintaining meaningful relationships is to advantage.

A key point to remember here is if quality relationships that lead to positive fulfillment aren't provided, that ugly void of emptiness can easily fill up with negative, which can only be counter-productive. "Keeping busy (or active)"—the Old Retirement's model mantra, is related to a increasing sense of aimlessness. Keeping busy works for a while, but with time, comes up short in terms of retirement contentment.

Adaptability

Seeking contentment is a pursuit of its own. It has much to do with our individual personalities, likes/dislikes, and proclivities, all of which take us back again to that need of genuine *self-identity*. If identity is clear, it's then a matter of channeling who we are in appropriate direction which suits us, and others, best. I mention others, for if we suit only ourselves, our attitudes can become myopic, to the chagrin of others, and likely coming back in displeasure toward us, ruining relationships.

The degree to which each of us possesses this quality trait of adaptability is highly complex in origin, and certainly also varies by degree among us. The more adaptable we are in all of life's situations, the better our chances of maintaining and developing healthy relationships, including during retirement.

The 'magic' solution involved here: *staying flexible.*

Staying emotionally flexible plays in directly with enjoying and maintaining quality relationships during the retirement years. We may well know our identity and have a clear understanding of how we'd like our outside relationships aligned, but we do well not to forget that retirement brings considerable, personal perspective change in ways that can influence, usually toward the negative, the clearest of personal retirement goals. It is in these conditions that adaptability is crucial. Why perspective changes? Because pressures of aging and related retirement strains can sour attitudes that were easily palatable in an earlier day. Disgruntlement and discontent stemming from myriad sources can negatively influence what once were of no consequence.

For example, chronic pain of worsening arthritis may make it more difficult to put on as genuine a happy face, thereby applying strain among personal inter-relations that used to be a non-consideration when ongoing pain wasn't an issue.

Well, you might ask, just how does one adapt well to life's continuing changes, aspects of life over which we have no control?

Adaptability is the graceful art and skill of adjusting ourselves, readily, to changing conditions. Simple enough, right? No, it's not a snap-the-fingers affair, is it. Adjusting ourselves to accommodate that to which we're not at all familiar takes some doing. Adaptableness involves emotive, educational, spiritual, and moral factors; probably more. It's a complex mix and topic of its own.

If, however, we know ahead of time (back to *planning and preparation*) that the chances of heightened adaptability being needed during retirement are great, we, now, can start to take inventory (back to *self-introspection*) and see if we discover personal traits that would do well with some adjustment.

Again, we don't want to wait until we're in retirement to begin working on developing adaptability!

One thing is certain, and this should propel us toward the goal of getting serious about obtaining more adaptability in our lives: Life change is as predictable as the sun rising tomorrow morning! We know it's inevitable. Dr. Johnson has a few suggestions for what I think he well calls developing a "... *willingness to embrace change.*" This willingness applies to any area of retirement life, not just to the Relationship Life Arena, although it's particularly applicable here. See if any of these contrasts of opposing human traits strike home. I quote:

> *... we need to develop skills that let us become more*
> *accepting rather than critical;*
> *more agreeable rather than argumentative;*
> *more forgiving rather than judging;*
> *more temperate rather than harsh;*
> *more at peace with ourselves and with the world rather*
> *than angry.*

From the above, it is all the more reinforced that each of us is responsible for doing our part in staging our retirement. Society won't do that for us, nor will preparation occur on its own. Too ridiculously fundamental? Indeed the concept of good preparation is utterly obvious, but the trick in getting *self* to put teeth to it, is another story. Self, have you noticed, has particular tendency to put off what it doesn't sense needs to be accomplished today.

Dealing with self—that's the next Life Arena to explore. If we don't have self under reasonable control, we live in relative chaos with ourselves. Retirement, as good as especially the new model can be, is fraught with the same life realism we experience throughout our lives. If we take a chaotic or imbalanced self into retirement, that last phase of life developmentalism simply will not improve on what's already messy.

24

Life Arena #4—Self

Self is a funny bird, isn't it? There's no one who knows self better than we, but often others see us, at least in some ways, more clearly than we do ourselves. Will paradox never cease?

The Self Arena, according to Dr. Johnson, is actually comprised of two parts. He breaks down "self" into two distinct categories:

- Self is considered the sum total of our relationship with our inward person: self-esteem; self-regard; self appraisal, etc.
- Self involves a close relationship with our bodies.

Self—Relationship with our Inner Person

Subjectivity is key here; it's not about how others see us, but how we see ourselves—our minds, soul, body and spirit. How we view ourselves determines how we live out these four components comprising our total make up.

Concerning how we live our lives in retirement has much to do with who we understand to be in control of our personhood. Interestingly, the Old Retirement model actually placed self in the lesser role of who controlled our retirement life direction.

Case in point, the old retirement model put society and employers more in control of when and how retirees would 'take retirement'. This is no degradation toward either; it simply illustrates the way in which society and retiree integrated. When certain age boundaries were reached, retirement policies and pension plans were put into effect. You took your gold watch and headed for whatever the 'rocking chair' meant to you.

Self's Options—for Today's Retiree

The New Retirement paradigm is much different. Today "self" is more in control of retirement decision making.

Although today's pre-retiree lives in a more flexible societal environment than that of previous generations, with that flexibility comes responsibility. More choice and options *doesn't* mean retirees make the best choices within this flexibility. As we've noted, although we generally retire earlier, live longer, have more money, and are healthier than our parents may have been, is not to say even the New Retirement model is bullet-proof; it's not. It's up to the individual retiree to *choose* either to produce quality post-career living or remain in the Old Retirement model concept of what comes, comes—the que sera, sera scenario.

Self is like good seed. Depending on where it gets planted in retirement will have much to do with the personal yield to be expected. Good soil usually bears well, but rocky and dry land causes good seed to wither and die. Retirees *are* good seed. We need to plant ourselves where we'll grow best.

Let's talk seed, soil and root.

Self's 'seed' needs to be planted in fields of hope and happiness. This is where self's seed takes root. No guarantees, however. Hope and happiness are fields known to be of inherently good quality, but lack of rain, wind or hail storms can ruin the best of intended crop planting, so to speak. Adversity we can't control; selection of the right soil, we can.

Because the seed of self is where we live, move, and have our being, it needs to be rooted in attributes of life that have origins in rightness, goodness, virtue and optimism, all of which are prime elements of hope and happiness.

I don't mean to be prudish or goody-two-shoes about this: I'm simply saying *as self sews, so does it reap.* Self needs to be

223

planted in good retirement soil—genuine optimism and hope. (It bears repeating and accentuation!)

Why is self-determination such as this so needed? This answer takes us back to Part I's explanations of sheer reality. One of life's certain realities (among many) means we do wither with time; aging and advancing time are no friends. As we view the withering of all things, however, we need to realize that although an end is inevitable, that end is not yet and much life remains. Does this not provide much reason for exercising hope along the timeline granted us?

We generally understand hope to be a sense or feeling that what is wanted can be had, or that events will turn out for the best. Involving hope with retirement, Dr. Johnson provides a particularly good application of the linkage. The outcome of what he says, which directly concerns self's positioning for retirement, provides positivism not only for the future retirement outlook, *but enhances happiness of today*. I find this profound, and therefore quote as follows:

Hope facilitates an attitude of ever-emerging happiness in your world today.... You may not have thought of your retirement preparation as an exercise in hope, but under closer analysis we come to see that hope is the undergirding value which gives us the motive power to continue on, inspired and in good cheer!

When we can rise to some level of hope in our own future, then we can multiply our happiness today. *If we fail to rise to hope, even at some rudimentary level, then we risk becoming despondent. Without hope we flounder and lose the will to live life to the fullest.... Without hope life eventually becomes simply dreaded.*

I think a most striking insight Dr. Johnson presents here is *happiness today* is somehow proportional to the degree of hope we can project into the future. This says as we look ahead with optimism, our *current* sense of well-being is amplified; conversely, if our forward vision is morose, that view has an immediate negative impact on our feelings today.

Adding to his point on multiplied happiness, I think back to the relationship between happiness and joy mentioned in an earlier chapter. Joy is deeper than happiness, rooted in more certain conviction and belief. Happiness is more circumstantial; i.e., if life is treating me well today, I'm happy. We need, therefore, to make hope reign eternal.

We can't really find joy in hope itself, because hope, by definition, lacks assuredness of what's desired. Joy is rooted in something counted on. For instance, *"I find great joy in antici-pating invigorating fall weather that ushers away the steaminess of summer."* In short—Hope and be happy!

In the Old Retirement model, we know that post-career 'soil' tended to produce poor yield of the good in life. It was (and still can be if current retirees choose to remain there) *negative* in nature, centered mostly in the idea that continued deterioration of the physical and mental self spelled degrada-tion to anything that lay ahead. Retirees were *conditioned* by culture and society—and certainly previous generations—to view late life as a non-directional, slowly withering away of what was once vibrant living. This is not to say retirees didn't enjoy retirement, but the general view of later-life wasn't par-ticularly hopeful and exciting.

Self—Relationship with our Bodies

The human physical frame is the *visible, tangible, vehicle* of life! Brimming and jam-packed with electronic and biologic activity, it's part of the premier Creation masterpiece we know to be us; you and me.

The physical body, being visible and tangible, is actually a shadow of what and who we really are. You and I, our real personhoods, are not what we see, handle, and put to physical use; the body is only the masterpiece facilitator that enables and expedites human thought and engagement (our soul di-mension) to be expressed in terms we understand to be human life on earth.

Interestingly, our brain isn't us either. It's a huge part of what we associate with self, but it's 'only' a fabricated tool that coordinates the actions of the body and engages use of the mind and its subcategories, intellect and understanding. (Feelings, emotions, and will are yet another part of self—we discussed them in Part One.)

225

And then there's our spiritual component. Our spirit is where connection with conscious life is made; it's that element of self that connects (some say mediates) between the body and soul.

Our issue here isn't about human origin, but it's good to establish some basis of the complexity that is "self". We need to have some orientation to what we actually think of our physical bodies. Why? Because the more we understand and marvel at our wondrous complexity, the more likely we will appreciate, and apply, self's bodily care in retirement.

Attending to the maintenance of physical health in retirement directly relates to retirement maximization, needless to say. But it *is* needful to say that many retirees see good physical health more along the lines of treating poor living habit's negative symptomatic results, rather than taking pro-active steps to, well, "stay in shape", avoiding many ill-symptoms in the first place. For example, far too many put self's relationship to the physical body into having decent health insurance that will pay for the never-ending treating of aging's aches, pains, and inner functional body ills with pharmaceutical symptom remedies. This may appear to be easier than enforcing personal, high quality eating and exercise programs, but is poor long-term planning. Easy, yes; qualitative, physical life retirement planning- *no*. Self's relationship to the physical body is something to which most retirees nod in agreement, but don't put into practice.

The Self Arena can't be cheated in later years. Body, soul, mind and spirit are an entity. Their function is as a car: you can limp along with one nearly flat tire, but getting to your destination sure won't be expedient or pleasant. Let the tire go completely flat and you stop where you are.

Body, soul, mind and spirit form who we are. The first three are more easily related in human thinking. Spirit, on the other hand, although directly influential in regard to soul and mind, is distinct and needs attention in its own mystical sphere; we'll look at the Spirit Life Arena, next.

25

Life Arena #5—Spirit

The last several paragraphs of the preceding chapter introduced self's most mysterious, sometimes puzzling quality—the realism of our spiritual dimension. Continual controversy and misunderstanding surround it.

Spirit is a difficult word to define. It's a literal entity that completely lacks material substance. Our spiritual dimension is an entity some sources imply mediates between body and soul. I like that idea because as we experience life, we sense an awareness of some element within us that relates to what we call conscience—the area of thought that mixes ethical, moral, *and* spiritual values.

Conscience and spirit aren't the same thing, but it appears they work in conjunction with one another, leading us to motive development, which ultimately causes the making of decisions. Of course, actions then follow decisions.

This isn't easy stuff, but it's part of who we are. For some, though not everyone, the better we understand how our thinking and general life activity are related, the more enabled we seem to be in day to day function. Others do better getting up in the morning, putting their feet on the floor, and taking on the day with little knowledge or concern about what makes them tick.

Experience has shown me that probably the ideal approach to conducting the best balance of life is possessing some knowledge of our makeup, but not being so dependent on analyzing it that we stifle ourselves in self-analyzation; balance and moderation, as with many things.

Is Spirit Real?

Many people deeply strive to delve into spiritual concepts. Some only regard spirituality as a necessary tack-on to life. Others appear to have no interest whatsoever, seeming to be entirely consumed with the secular, the physical. Then there are some who blatantly refute and deny existence of intangibles, such as our spirit.

Before we look further into life's Spirit Arena, let's see if we can establish some credibility toward the existence of a spiritual dimension within us, for if we have no belief such an entity exists and is part of who we are, there's little reason to go further with spiritual discussion.

Intangible entities are realities just as are tangible ones. But how do we know these intangibles exist if we have no tangible proof they do? Their existence is proven by the observable *effects* they make.

For example—wind, pain, electricity, love, loss, and many other intangibles are every bit as real as physical, tangible entities. Trees bending proves the invisible existence of wind (moving, hot/cold, invisible air). This is a truth-filled reality. There are many more examples: rushing to the dentist with an abscessed tooth evidences the truth-filled reality of pain; touching a 'hot' electrical wire reveals pain *and* electricity in the same real sense; being greatly moved by another's loving deeds, or crying over deep personal loss, surely verify the truthfulness and literal presence of invisible emotions.

Spiritual reality, therefore, can be compared, at least in principle, to other intangibles we do not see with our eyes nor observe directly by our senses.

A Difficult Chapter to Write

Why the difficulty? First, discussion on spirituality directly connects to the 'God' issue, a scenario ripe for controversy, as neither God nor spirituality is easily defined.

Secondly, I want to be able to write *clearly* on what I *mean to say*, something often harder to do than realized, especially on such an abstract topic.

Third, I sincerely don't want to offend anyone by appearing to pry into some of the deepest segments of our being—areas where our personal considerations of God dwell if, in fact, we see God to be part of fundamental Truth concerning life in the first place.

I ask kindly of you, therefore, as you read this chapter to understand the genuineness of my intent; that is, to discuss the difficult without fear I'm offending someone, and for the reader to receive my thoughts in the spirit (no pun intended) of humility and sincerity in which they are offered.

Developing Positive Appreciation of Spiritual Reality

Obviously, the entirety of the book you are holding, *Retirement's Missing Link,* isn't centered in faith and spiritual issues. Spirituality, or the lack of it, however, powerfully influences all phases of our lives—from early/mid-childhood until death. Our perception of the spiritual, its accompanying faith, and how we react to each spill over and affect *all other life's* arenas: career, family, relationships, perception of self, and leisure. Spirituality centers in our self's life arena most of all, providing profound influence on how self is directed both in everyday life and in terms of eternity.

Spirituality cannot be escaped; ignored maybe. Even if we claim to have no faith in anything we understand to be spiritual, we are paradoxically exercising faith that nothing spiritual exists. At bottom line, spiritual reality is as integral to life as our bodies and the earth upon which we walk. It's as real as the invisible air we breathe—*unseen* for sure, but as necessary for life as all the physical attributes much more easily understood.

Spirit can be recognized as an important factor that separates humans from animals. Although it can be argued animals have souls, they don't have the capacity to conceive or relate to abstract reality such as contemplating why we are here, the meaning of life, the understanding there is power greater than ourselves, and so on.

Why Our Spiritual Reality is So Important

There's no question about or disagreement among humans there is obviously something about our humankind that dramatically differentiates us from lower forms of animal life.

The Animal Kingdom doesn't have capacity for personal peace, stability, planning ahead or a multitude of other characteristics common to humans. Animals do, of course, possess *physical* characteristics we don't; specialization that's utterly astounding. So why the divide; why this spiritual entity that sets us apart from the physical wonders that surround us?

A direct relationship can be drawn here: the more inner personal peace, stability, and orderliness we possess, the greater our total personality makeup positively affects all other areas of life. If this sense of inner balance and well-being is present, indicating our "spirit is at rest" (one way we verbally understand inner peace to be expressed), then most all we touch in life—family, relationships, our work, even our leisure life will be enhanced. Of course, this also directly applies to our retirement experience as well. In fact *every* phase of life benefits if the "spirit is at rest"—in our youth, mid-life career stage, retirement, and old age.

Frankly, during the boomer's pre-retirement life stages, the clutter of life more easily can mask sensitivity to spiritual concerns. Once many of the trappings, supports, materialism, and hide-behinds of life fall away—during later retirement and into serious old age—a more intense benefit of having spiritual life in order is most appreciated. And needed!

It's at that time we are figuratively naked. Life and death are viewed in much more stark terms. We know we've mostly lived life and have death and eternity before us; it's a time to *seriously* exercise the goodness of a right spirit within us.

Regardless of our developmental stage of life stemming from youth through old age, a spiritual life in good condition is usually an indicator of virtuous living characterized by relative moral excellence. If our spiritual nature is in harmony with total self, overall, we live in relative inner peace, producing extended virtue to all we touch—a *priceless* commodity to ourselves and others.

Unfortunately, the inverse relationship also applies: weak, negative, or no sense of spiritual reality translates into a life that's, on some levels, counter-productive to all that's good. This is not to say a person with little or no sense of personal spiritual reality is more 'evil' than a spiritually sensitive individual; both groups of people—as we all know—clearly lead imperfect lives. It only means the *chances of producing* inner peace and living a relatively virtuous life dwindle, opposed to the results of one who understands an indwelling spiritual realism and takes it seriously.

The Consequences of Minimizing Spiritual Realism

Many people, in at least a cursory manner, will acknowledge a degree of belief in spiritual reality. Although they at least tangentially believe, a glib, indecisiveness seems to lurk in the background. They don't find the spiritual especially essential or central to daily life—sort of a take-it-or-leave-it-concept. Most say they believe in a spiritual God, may pray, maybe attend church or other sort of religious assembly, but mainly, on an everyday basis, just get on with life in a practical, self-directed manner.

This having a form of spirituality, but not exercising it in everyday life, is common. It's a stand-offish yet inquisitive approach—rooted in spiritual indecision and indifference—and is hallmark to much of humanity. It's especially prevalent in much of the boomer population whose main life focus is definitively on the material.

If our lives are governed by less than a strong sense of virtuous, spiritual guidance, what are the results? In fact, these results might be better called consequences because they are negative.

When meaningful spiritual reality lacks, a double-minded wobbliness about the whole of life reality arises. In other words, it opens the door to a sometimes excessive concentration on unsettling questions: What's real and what isn't? How can I know? *Who* knows...? Who *cares*! This progression is dangerous because it leaves us open to buying into most any wind of spiritual doctrine and thinking that may come along. Having weak or no spiritual root also leads to thinking life is unsolvable and ultimately futile.

Spiritual uncertainty also creates inner restlessness. If restlessness lies within the deepest aspect of our being, at the very least, this creates a perpetual drain on our emotions. This drain may be low key, even indiscernible, but if we allow a mix of confusion and indecision to worsen, it easily develops into anxiety, hopelessness, depression, and even despair. (Depression is the chief malady of retirees.)

Having no strong spiritual foundation is like experiencing an empty gas tank on the road of life, in a snowstorm....

The Spiritual Gas Tank

Think of being on a lightly traveled road in a snow storm. The fuel gauge is registering near empty because, for one reason or another, you put off stopping for gas when passing fill-up opportunities earlier in the trip.

Your destination at this point in your travel isn't far, but at this late time you realize there's not enough gas remaining to get you to it. Minute to minute that knot in the stomach intensifies. You are tense, as a sickly sense of guilt sets in because you didn't stop for gas when you could have done so. Confusion of what to do starts to rise. The tension affects your entire disposition—your sense of virtue begins to diminish. That person riding in the car with you begins to worry and becomes upset as well, for you begin revealing yourself as tense, up-tight, and very unhappy. Again, you angrily ask yourself why you weren't more attentive to the developing *void* in that blasted gas tank earlier, when you had opportunity to fill up!

Sincerely being rooted in genuine spiritual reality can be the fuel that helps us complete the road trip of life, snowstorms and all.

Suggestion to all pre-retirees of *any* age, boomers, and even current retirees: we are all traveling this road of life, and no snowstorm may be in the immediate forecast—clear and sunny, it may be, but don't be mislead and lazy. Fill the spiritual gas tank, now, while you have opportunity:

If it's too much trouble to stop for fuel now, think how much more difficult it will be to do so if a snowstorm of life settles in unexpectedly during retirement and later years. Procrastinators put off at their own peril, and all too often at the expense of others.

Our overall destination in this book journey is to transition into retirement *prepared and possessing a general sense of inner equilibrium and personal orderliness.* Sound spirituality is a powerful life stabilizer in that regard; we do well to give it serious attention.

Plant Now; Reap Later

The reality of our spiritual life, because it's so private, can be a touchy subject to discuss. But even though it's very personal, it's also crucial to our overall well-being. Who of us likes going to a doctor and be told blood pressure levels need adjustment? We don't like it, but should be glad levels can be measured and that there are means of lowering hypertension.

Does any of this spiritual talk make sense to you? Do you think this issue of spirituality has any real effect on people's lives or, instead, it's one of those churchy things 'religious' people like to talk about and doesn't really affect you at all?

Whether or not you believe each of us possesses a sense of spirituality depends on several things:

1. Your upbringing and life exposure certainly have provided a spiritual/non-spiritual baseline.

2. If you've never heard much about spirituality, you may have little or no opinion of the topic; maybe it's real, maybe not. Maybe you don't tend to think about such things in the first place. Or you may think who cares about any of it anyway.

3. Maybe you somehow believe spirituality is a real dimension of your being, but don't consider it a big deal in life, so it's ignored. It's easy to reason that with all life's physical and mental demands—who needs to be concerned with spiritual concepts as well!

4. On the other hand you may possess serious spiritual commitment to the point that your spirituality is the prime basis of your daily existence.

Taking the time to get spiritual root planted will bring life yield in due time. It's like taking the effort to plant a seedling tree early, only to see it mature into producing much fruit.

Planning now to get your spiritual person in good stead can, therefore, only *increase* your retirement experience. It's a matter of priority and order.

Get the spiritual void filled if it's not already, and the important things of life are not only more obtainable, but more maximized.

We know the idea of planning toward and preparing for retirement is to maximize all the opportunity it holds when it finally arrives. Having a right spirit within us is directly proportional to that success.

Filling the Spiritual Void

A "spiritual void" is what we might think of as an empty container, like an empty soup bowl waiting for some wonderful French Onion soup, for example. It's designed and perfectly fit for holding something, but if it holds nothing of value it's worthless in relation to the reason it was created. (Interestingly, every void really isn't a complete emptiness. Our empty soup bowl example actually contains something—air, but air isn't worth much when it comes to spiritual hunger: "Where's the soup"?!)

Unless it's filled with material for which it's been designed, for all intents the container (our capacity for spiritual fullness) is empty and useless. Our spirits are designed to be filled with faith and sensitivity that draws us close to the spiritual component reality we individually acknowledge; i.e., God, higher power, spirit, etc. Of course this assumes we do so acknowledge such existence in the first place.

The soup bowl (filled with air) idea illustrates that *something* will fill the spiritual void even if what's doing the filling (air) is inappropriate or worthless. In fact, there's no such thing as spiritual vacuums; *something* fills the void. The human tendency is to *substitute* true spiritual in-filling *with all sorts of alternatives*—materialism, keeping busy, flitting from interest to interest, being lost in personal enjoyment or even quality fulfillment activities toward both self and others. All these vie for prominence in providing what we believe to be life satisfaction. And to a point they do, but because our spirit component isn't designed for anything but connectivity to the spiritual, for all practical purposes we come up short.

I trust I'm clear on this. What fills the spiritual void is not the same as day to day activity, but is as important—even more so. The point here is that *two* elements are involved:

1. soul activity—everyday thinking and resultant living that motivates all our activity, good and bad

2. spirit activity—which is, or should be, the motivating force behind what the soul lives out, day to day.

My aim is to certainly acknowledge and promote worthwhile and fulfilling everyday life activity, but to *also* recognize that continually seeking after life's day to day doings is fleeting *and is found lacking* if not rooted in something more fundamentally deep, even eternal. That 'something' has to do with the spiritual dynamic of life itself.

Have you ever wanted, wanted, *so* wanted something? If *only* you could get that one thing you'd 'be happy'! Finally, you got that heart's desire, but before long, the luster wore off—the object of desire satisfied temporarily, but soon that old pattern of yearning for something more, something new, returned. And the pattern repeats:

Thusly is a major life void defined.

It's as if we keep filling a leaky bucket with water. It takes fixing the leak that causes the voiding of water. Spiritually, this means coming to terms with reality by realizing our attainment of materialism, and even experiencing general life fulfillment, as good and even virtuous as these might be, doesn't get the spiritual bucket plugged. There's something more.

It appears that we are designed so nothing of this world, materially, provides lasting peace—try as we may. It appears this occurs because part of our inherent design is to have relationship, albeit unseen and spiritually oriented, with our Creator. In other words, a yearning *is designed within us* that only can be filled with a spiritual element.

[Isn't it interesting the Holy Scriptures (Bible) actually *defines* God *as Spirit*; specifically, '*God is Spirit...*'- John 4:24. This means He is a non-material, personal being, completely self-conscious and self-determining.]

Based on the above scripture verse, if on nothing else, doesn't it make sense that all of us have some level of spiritual sensitivity and yearning within us? If God is spirit, would it not make sense that his Creation (you and me) would have some built-in sense of spiritual capacity and connectivity— yes, (to the skeptic), even if it can't be 'proven' and is invisible?

We are given pleasure to be found in many material things and life events, but none have ongoing staying power to satisfy continually.

Ultimate life satisfaction is to be found *past* the material and the mundane; *past* what we can eke out of physical life as we know it.

Each of us, in varying ways, tries to fill life's seemingly instinctual desire for peace and fulfillment. It's interesting that regardless of how close any of us come to that goal, or at least rationalize we do, none of us can claim a lasting, immovable peace, based on daily life and the materialism that supports it. There has to be more....

Without getting deeper into theology, the basics of this dilemma are rooted in the fact that mankind lives in a fallen-from-perfection world (have you noticed?). A fallen world is one in which paradisiacal perfection *could* have been the rule, but isn't. This is ground zero: where we all live. Welcome to paradise fallen....

What is *most* important here, in our study relating spirituality to retirement and aging, is:

1. To recognize the importance of "spirit" among Dr. Johnson's six broad Life Arena categories, and to reiterate that these arenas apply to all stages (phases) of life, which obviously includes the pre-retirement, mid-life career stage as well as retirement.

   [Note: In my presentation on the spiritual I have to assume my readers aren't already seriously involved with the spiritual connection to life. Of course, many may well so be. For you, may the above offer some relevant, qualitative review.]

2. To soberly acknowledge that how we are spiritually wired during the career years will be carried directly into our retirements, so it's especially important to consider some solid spiritual foundation during the pre-retirement preparatory period.

Were I writing a treatise on spirituality at this time in my life, but I'm not, I'd be writing an apologetic (a rational support) for Christianity. It would center on why I believe:

- mankind (man) has been created by an infinite, all-powerful God
- man has fallen from the graces of that God through man's will to satisfy self rather than maintain a perfectly holy relationship with his Creator
- man must choose to accept or reject forgiveness and rec-

onciliation with his Creator (to do nothing is to remain in a fallen, in an unreconciliatory state)
• man has opportunity to be restored to a loving and redeemed standing with the Creator who made him.

Obviously, however, this book is not one centering on why I believe Christianity is the answer to mankind's overall spiritual dilemma. I'm so convinced the linkage between man's fallen condition and a Holy God is valid, however, a short book on such may be in my future. Not to say the field of Christian apologetic publication isn't amply filled—it is. The entirety of Christianity is so unending in scope, though, maybe there always room for one more voice.

So…, without veering off on beliefs I hold particularly dear (thanks for listening), we'll concentrate on some benefits of our spirituality, but not slanted toward or away from any particular faith or denomination. General spiritual growth, whatever your persuasion, can be helpful during any phase of life development, retirement and increased aging most certainly included—for obvious reasons.

Disclaimer (of sorts): The writing of the above paragraphs opens up a universe of discussion, debate, and controversy. We won't get deeply into comparative religion or theories of existence and origins here, as much as I'd like to. My aim is to only suggest that we all have a yearning for 'something more' in life *which is integrally involved especially in retirement and the aging process.*

Benefits of Being Spiritually Minded

Spirituality, in a very broad sense, and as applied to everyday living has much to do with growing out of wrong beliefs and concepts and into thoughts that ever increase the good of our relationship to the world around us and, to many, to relationship to whatever it is we understand as being a higher authority over us.

As mentioned, in this particular discussion I'm attempting to side-step anything that touches on religious affiliation.

Instead we are centering more on whatever it is you understand as the spiritual element of your being, and realizing how important that element is in coordinating with the other elements of your total Life Arena: career, family, relationships, self, and leisure.

First and foremost is the personal acknowledgment that *your prime essence is spirit*, which happens to travel around in a mortal, physical frame—your body. At first blush, my guess is that this concept seems strange; most people think body is prime, then soul, mind and spirit are somehow crammed into the physical. In other words, the physical *seems* to take precedence over all the rest.

There are fundamentally several reasons spirit is the core essence of who we are, but to get into a discussion on this here would lead us into theology and philosophy, neither of which are applicable to our central theme of retirement and aging. Pages, and pages—another topic for another time.

So then….What are some benefits of engaging spirituality within our being?

- Spiritual sensitivity has a way of increasing self-awareness, that sense of who we are and our place and purpose in life. If all of life is spent flitting from one activity to another, self-awareness can't develop. We need to stop : "smell the roses", and grow in understanding of how we inwardly relate to the world around us. By so doing, we turn our spiritual eyes toward God, or whatever/whoever we construe our understanding of a higher power to be. This accomplishes an increased responsiveness to our deity, creating within us good, positive manner of general thinking. Finally, as our thinking focus is made more qualitative, our general life direction takes on finer elements of meaning and fulfillment.

On a more specific benefit level, being spiritually-minded helps us detach from the din around us, leading to inner peace:

- External circumstances, that usually have profound influence on mood and state of mind, are better held in check.

- Rising above disappointment and its accompanying frustration and negative feelings improves.
- Our ability to discern between right and wrong, good and evil is heightened.
- Inner power and strength are enhanced.
- We become more tolerant and patient.
- All in all, when we assign ourselves (a volitional choice) to be spiritually alive, good is the usual result.
- Some cynics may say all this about the spiritual aspects of life is nonsense; i.e., "It's all in your head". I say, let the results stand for themselves. Literal proof of the spiritual connection may or may not be existent, but if the results of spiritual emphasis yield a more quality life, argument of literal spiritual validity is moot, don't you think?

Spiritual Contrasts; Spiritual Peace

It's a crisp fall day, mid-afternoon; I've returned to my writing. Before lunch, I'd finished working on this chapter concerning spirituality, pondering deeply thoughts I'd written.

Sun shines through the curtain lace as if to further enhance the delight I find in penning ideas having to do with God, our spirits, and eternity. It's as bright as can be; reassuring me life is full of splendid wonder, even though full comprehension of it all is beyond human reach. Such contrast; such wonder.

I've also just came back from a walk to the cemetery. At first you might think the juxtaposition of the all the brightness of the sunlight's goodness alongside the heaviness and relative gloom of the word cemetery to be odd. Contrasts are impactful and revealing, as I'll describe....

Within close walking distance to our home in the country is a small, old, church family cemetery situated under giant oaks and maples, and probably dating back to the early 1700s. A bit ago, our granddaughter, for whom we frequently babysit, came in my study and asked if we could take a walk to the cemetery. She's three. The enormous trees within the cemetery stand as sentinels over the deceased; she loves to walk among the fallen acorns, talk up a storm, and then return home.

When at the cemetery, I always look at old dates and names. Most of the writing is in German and dates back so far the dates are gone with the wind. Many small children markers dot the rows as well—a most poignant statement in contrasts as Alida skips and plays. The stark reality of our temporal dwelling place on earth, elicited by those stone emblems of physical death, always bring me to a point of profound wonder and awe: how does the absolute *mystery* of it all work? The wearing-away of chiseled words by the elements over time only intensify the reality of transitory man. Even more poignant, it's late October. Today, against a bold blue sky with white puffs, autumn leaves continued to let go of their attachment to life, drifting earthward to gently rest among the dwelling places of the faithful, now departed.

Seeing the bud of youth frolic amid the fallen leaves and rows of quiet markers finalized the certain profoundness of the moment, all the more putting into vivid contrast the mystery we know as physical existence, then departure.

We returned home having gathered handfuls of fallen acorns as a memento of our walk together. I'm back at the keyboard, and still taking note of time well spent....

Where does this precious sentiment lead me? It leads to that place in my innermost recesses where a spiritual peace lays quietly, an assurance of life past the emptiness of the grave. It's a **spiritual peace** that can take me through retirement with hope—that wonderful life ingredient, by contrast, which gives meaning to the physical brevity that cemeteries so vividly represent. And because of hope in the future, rooted in what I've come to conclude to be Truth, today is made happier than it could otherwise possibly be.

May I suggest—

If you don't have committed spiritual views, now's a fine time to seek and find.

Whatever the outcome of your spiritual searching, my sincerest wish is for fulfillment in the object of your finding.

May it richly *bless and enhance all other Life Arena aspects* as you continue to mature in your retirement life developmental phase.

Should you have more sincere interest in substantive, genuine Christianity and would like discussion about it, do feel free to contact me, personally, via the email connection on my website: www.personal-retirement-planning.com.

26

Life Arena #6 —Leisure

Back in Chapter 20 we began probing the six of Dr. Johnson's Life Arenas: Career; Family; Relationships; Self; Spirit; Leisure. We noted all of daily life, throughout our entire lives, operates within one or more of these spheres of life activity. Because this is where each of us lives all of life, these arenas provide a perfect *functional structure* for formulating a personal retirement life plan.

The last of these six is *leisure*. In Part I of this book, I lambasted our culture's excessive retirement emphasis on finances and leisure as being highly disproportional to other deep aspects of real life retirement importance. Of course, leisure and retirement are, in fact "horse and carriage" in the retirement context—no argument there. The trick, however, is to keep leisure and fun *in good balance with more weighty issues of life reality*—and that's precisely what neither 'Wall Street' nor 'Main Street' delivers.

The Leisure Life Arena focuses on a retirement idea which is able to deliver relaxation in a way that brings about an *expanded* involvement in life rather than, as the Old Retirement model suggests—just relax, have fun, and exist.

In Dr. Johnson's book *The New Retirement*, he well states, and I quote:

> *The old retirement paradigm saw* (and continues to this day) *retirees entering a life of leisure; the new Retirement paradigm sees retirees entering a leisurely lifestyle.*

I'm dead serious when I suggest that most boomers look to retirement through freedom/fun goggles! A Certified Finan-

cial Planner, with whom I work closely, tells me the mantra he
hears incessantly from clients so typifies the Old Retirement
attitude. When asked what it is about retirement that beckons
most, the answer is something to the effect *'the ability to do
whatever it is you want to do, whenever you want to do it'*. Now
that's a catchy phrase alright, but is limited to an Old Retirement, narrow, retiree perspective. Deep down, if you really get
to talk with many of these retirees, a nagging sense of emptiness surfaces, revealing only a half-baked actuality of real life
fulfillment.

New Retirement paradigm thinking means truly finding
outlets which promote recognition and implementation of our
leisure needs. One of the best ways to coral such self-attrib-
utive traits is via the RSP (Retirement Success Profile). The
profile isn't magic, but it creates an alert awareness of specific,
individual traits and attitudes you can pursue, some of which
you may not have thought of for years, if ever. It creates trigger
points that get you thinking outside the ubiquitous 'box'—
that place your mind tends to take permanent resident, sometimes at the expense of brand new ideas.

Regardless of how retirement leisure is sliced, it's a well-
deserved fulfillment of a life need: we age and need a break!
Common knowledge tells us, and our bodies signal, that no
leisure; i.e., no break, is counterproductive to balanced, enjoyable living.

Dr. Johnson makes a particularly interesting leisure commentary. Again, I quote:

Paradox of Leisure

*One of the paradoxes of leisure is that for an activity
to be leisure it must be diversion; a vacation, a
breather, a break, a new space. If we take-on the
old retirement role, making leisure the central, and
perhaps the only focus of our lives, we risk not having
any leisure at all. When leisure becomes the primary
focal point of living, it ceases to provide the essential
pleasure and rejuvenation that it is intended to
provide. Leisure loses its luster when it takes central
stage in our lives. The paradox of leisure is that it*

must remain secondary to what is the primary focus of our life if it is to retain its ability to refresh us. What is primary in the new retirement paradigm is pursuing our dream. There may be overlap between our leisure and our life dream in that pursuing our dream may be pleasurable, fun, and fulfilling; yet we must take a breather, break from, and vacate even from our dream if we wish to remain committed to it, and if we hope to continue to receive the full measure of fulfillment that is there for us.

Leisure Benefits

Until pre-retirees finally make the move into retirement, definitions of leisure barely suffice. I say this because so much of career life is about anything but leisure. Of course, everyone in career life experiences leisure times, but it's not until the capability to experience deeper leisure arrives during retirement that the term can take on full meaning. Channeled into qualitative avenues, leisure is not only a catharsis to the individual, but can be highly beneficial to others.

Enter, again, the New Retirement. Pre-retirees who get to the point of realizing retirement is vastly more positive and fulfilling than the older disengagement mentality are in much better position to find retirement leisure as a vehicle leading to an enriched participation of body, mind, and soul stimulation.

The New Retirement oriented pre-retiree lives less the self-centric existence and more one engaged in life's vibrancy, whatever that may mean to the individual. Leisure is recognized as being stimulating and engaging, both in genuinely fulfilling self activities and those involving others.

BENEFITS OF STIMULATING LEISURE:

- *Personal values*—Stimulating leisure allows time for examination of personal values—to determine and focus on what is important for today and the years ahead.

245

- *Opportunity to really live*—stimulating leisure involves *you living instead of watching someone else live!* Being active and not a coach-potato/TV-aholic. By so doing, fulfilling activity takes the mind and body to places that cause *you* to really live instead of watching others enjoy life via the tube. (I realize we all have different temperaments and metabolisms, and mean no belittlement or condemnation toward retirees who prefer, say, TV watching more active lifestyles. What I mean to imply is only to consider that, generally, because we are healthier, retire earlier, and have more financial means than did our parents, the 'new retiree' is in far better position to act on such availabilities, should one be so inclined.)
- *Improved whole health*—the Old Retirement concept of disengaged leisure (more or less just 'hangin' around or performing likable, repetitive activity) most often leads not to improved health but the opposite. Disengaged leisure is characterized by busyness or repetitive ho-hum activity.

For instance, getting together with the 'guys' every Tuesday morning at the local fast food stop for coffee, donuts, and chatter is enjoyable, but obviously doesn't enhance an aging physical frame, might we say…. This is not to imply getting with the guys is in any means negative. But if leisure retirement life is *limited* to such level of activity, so is a direct correlation to improving aging health. One of New Retirement persuasion might be more of a mind to improve health by actively getting the boys to engage in low-key sports or exercise fun times that do stimulate ongoing physical health.

To restate, the disengagement mentality—the thinking that, "Ah… I've finally arrived to retirement where it's almost my duty to kick back and let life go by"—can be detrimental to body and mind. I find most early retirees think that for all the years of hard work they put it, now—at last (!) they will make up for all the times, during career, they never could really engage times of genuine leisure.

Frankly, *I endorse a time of extended, kick-back leisure upon early retirement!* There needs to be that release from the decades of rigorous work activity that held stranglehold on prime leisure for so long. Enjoy!!! But it's the big picture of *extended* retirement with which we must assure that quality leisure adds to overall health—of both body and mind.

Keep in mind that there are no vacuums in life: when one thing vacates a space, something else must fill it. Retirement leisure patterns should be established to the positive degree that they engage your full person, for the better of the whole. At all costs, leisure patterns that oppose depressive lethargy and physical deterioration are to be the aim.

- *Socialization*—during retirement, having more time opens the door to socialization and community barely possible during the work years. During the career years our work provides an internal (job-related) networking of continued socialization on varied levels.

As the transition is made into retirement living, care must be taken to assure socialization networking isn't abandoned. To reiterate: the Old Retirement model is classic for social deterioration! Retirees usually lose some or many of the relationships and friendships the on-the-job lifestyle perpetually promoted. What then? Maybe the fast food joint crowd replaces the old gang to some degree, but with such there surely are limitations. Such limitations can be a good instigator for developing meaningful life roles.

- *Meaningful life roles*—that couldn't have been possible earlier (due to career and life demands) are ever so possible during retirement. These can range from giving of self to help others to starting a brand new personal career or business! Again, the object is to be pro-active (New Retirement thinking) as opposed to anything that opens the door to depression and whole life deterioration.

An Unhealthy Resolution:

A "bleak landscape", Dr. Johnson calls a life without leisure. I fully agree with his assessment for I've experienced it personally. As well, so many pre-retirees *and* retirees run to and fro at breakneck pace, one wonders if they have any conception of the meaning of the very word.

I'll close this chapter quoting Dr. Johnson's well stated "Unhealthy Resolution"—

Life without leisure can create a bleak psychological landscape indeed. Our life without leisure quickly becomes anemic. When we can't, or don't position ourselves to receive the magnificent benefits leisure can bring we find we cannot reflect on the meaning of our lives. We come to be self-centered, our life degenerates into an unhealthy routine of simply "doing things." We lose our ability to appreciate the present moment. We eventually start to become callous, anxious, and self-absorbed. Developing a leisure attitude, the sense that we are seeing beauty all the time, gives us the pause to be grateful, and grants the most wonderful gift of all… serenity.

At this point we have explored the six arenas of life in which we all live, move, and have our being: career, family, relationships, self, spirit, and leisure. Because all we do in life involves these functional areas, if an individual were able to analyze self in each arena, what a helpful, composite picture would emerge concerning the person's overall relationship to a personal retirement blueprint, as it were.

The good news is—the RSP (Retirement Success Profile) is the analytical tool that can accurately produce the boomer's pre-retirement blueprint, or profile, as its name implies. We'll explore the RSP in the next chapter.

27

Where to Go from Here

Enter: the RSP (Retirement Success Profile)

Scattered throughout the book I've made references to the RSP because it is so instrumental in revealing important information feedback to the pre-retiree or current retiree reader, for that matter.

The RSP came into existence as over the years Dr. Johnson's gerontological and psychological research led him to fifteen prime factors that together constitute the content for a thorough retirement self-analysis. The RSP is a dedicated *retirement* profile that requires its user to seek within; that is, to commit to keen introspection that probably hasn't been attempted in years, maybe never. Dr. Johnson's comment on his RSP is sobering, and I quote:

> *This self-inventory is crucial if a new retirement lifestyle* (the New Retirement paradigm) *is to emerge; failure to undergo such a personal assessment leaves one at great risk for descending into the grip of the old retirement* (the Old Retirement paradigm).

He is correct. Because our societal culture incessantly insists retirement is all about finances, fun, and leisure, unless the boomer takes decisive action to expand on such narrow thinking, what are the chances of avoiding the Old Retirement mentality?

Dr. Johnson recommends doing the RSP self-evaluation in successive intervals: fifteen years, ten years, five and one year prior to anticipated actual retirement. He states this sort of progressive analysis can pay rich dividends by keeping your goals, life purpose, and personal fulfillment fresh. As well, it keeps your energies focused on what's truly important.

About the RSP (Retirement Success Profile)

FACTS ABOUT THE RSP:

The RSP, as described by Dr. Johnson himself, "*is a 120 item self-assessment that provides a detailed, personal inventory of your current strengths, as well as areas needing focus.*"

Once the RSP is completed, results are summarized and provide "*an accurate and comprehensive picture of your overall level of readiness for personal change and renewal*"—the state of affairs retirement will surely involve.

This "level of readiness" systematically analyzes your overall retirement readiness by 1) comparing your scores to approximately 50,000 others, like yourself, who have taken the RSP, and 2) by comparing *your own* individual scores of present behavior to levels you actually expect of yourself. Because of the ingenious design of the RSP, the 120 items you answer reveal your genuine self-expectations *and* how well you currently are measuring up to them. If this isn't a true life retirement indicator, I don't know what is.

The questions in the RSP directly relate to the six life arenas. In so doing, your responses ultimately form a pattern revealing that 'real you' we've talked so much about in the chapters. You begin to see your strengths, weaknesses, and aspects of life that are important to you. All this pulls together in helping you develop a personal retirement agenda that fits you, and you alone.

There are no right or wrong answers in the RSP, but your responses are strong indicators about how you deeply feel about retirement in general, and about how your own retirement transition in particular.

Your RSP *cannot* tell you when to retire, but it lets you know how well you are and are not prepared for the demands and complexities it will bring.

It needs to be clearly understood that the RSP is not a 'personality profile' in traditional terms. Although it certainly reveals aspects of your personal thinking, that thinking is *specifically related to making the transition from career to retirement only*. Many personal and career profile mechanisms are on the market that may help personally and vocationally, but *the RSP is retirement-target-specific*.

The RSP has been built on extensive research. In fact, its concept "… *was ten years in the research phase alone before it was released for public distribution. The RSP has seen three major field testings and revisions. It has proven itself an invaluable planning tool for persons addressing the mature career/life change of Renewal*." (Dr. Richard Johnson)

Bottom line—it works:

What you need most to build a successful retirement is information—*information about you!*

HOW THE RSP IS ADMINISTERED:

1. You can register for the RSP by going to my website: www.personal-retirement-planning.com The sign-up is easy and fast. You then receive the RSP material and complete it online.

2. The RSP results then come to me for analysis. I then personally analyze all resulting data in preparation for personal, in-depth, consultation with you by phone, concerning all the results.

3. It is from there you truly begin to pull together who you are in relation to your own retirement. I will help, guide, and coach, but *you* build your own retirement future. You'll find the entire process highly satisfying because you have pursued what no one else can do for you—forge your own future retirement agenda.

Maybe best of all, you will have accomplished what the boomer herd never gets 'round to doing—you will have found:

Retirement's Missing Link.

CHAPTER 28

EPILOGUE

Life Seasons

Is it late summer, fall, or early winter in your life? How do you know? In your thinking, has the 'season changed' since you began reading this book? Do you now sense yourself to be in a different relationship to your upcoming retirement event? Has that event taken on a looming or beckoning posture? Are you more anxious or more relieved?

The changing of the seasons, meaning those of life or nature's own, can illustrate something we all experience but usually miss because we're too busy living life. Time moves so slowly yet, ironically, so quickly the two seem to negate each other, causing time to practically stand still in what we know as the present. What's really going on is that ever so consistently we are progressing, seamlessly, and almost indifferently, from one life developmental stage—one season—to the next. Nature works similarly, of course, reinforcing the wonder of it all.

Nature's seasons have been circling for eons of time, offering proof it all somehow holds together. Each, at its elusive beginning and ending, has the ability and quality of *blending* into the preceding season or the one to follow. So it is with our developmental life stages. We change from childhood to adolescence, to mid-life, then to old age, but 'between' each of these main life segments, a blending, transitional period invisibly occurs.

SPRING AND SUMMER

In the spring of our lives we are broadly schooled. Then summer applies that learning to bring about the accomplishments we generally know as life experience, goals, achievements; the things of which life is comprised. In a very real physical sense, spring and summer are the seasons of life when 'production' ascends, then maintains.

The fervor and production of the summer season eventually wanes, giving way to fresh, cool and invigorating days, where focus shifts to the blessing of coolness and a respite from the rat race, heat, and exhaustion summer has produced. Without the summer season, though, no fall color could be possible: the bud; the blossom, the leaf, the fruit—and then the color. The process is intrinsically bound in design past finding out, it's glory maybe only exceeded by glorious color!

Entering the fall season, we find a dying to summer and new life in autumnal peace. The invisibleness of time has silently ushered away summer heat, allowing entrance of fall's refreshing. It can't be any other way, even should we so desire.

So it is. Because of the unyielding constraints and power of time—that intangible we have neither created nor over which we have any control, we witness the paradox of death to one entity giving life to another—as one season ends, another is born; the passing of one thing brings life to another.

In such, encouragement can be found, for as goes the migration of the seasons, so goes the transition of our beings: from one life developmental stage to the next.

FALL INTO WINTER

Fall, late fall especially, in the natural world brings with it dramatic changes. These changes starkly parallel those experienced in later life. Winter wind's falling leaf will render the landscape barren as snow descends as if to possess the earth, bringing a certain finality to summer breeze and September song.

Certainly there is loss.

Trees stand as naked reminders of an earlier time. The previous greens and subsequent autumnal tones have given way to a stark landscape. Things are seen clearly now, for what they are.

This *could* be a time of encroaching despair. Remembering Paul Simon's music of the sixties, I think of his then observant analysis of life's profound reality:

> *"I threw a pebble in a brook, and watched the ripples run away. And they never made a sound. And the leaves that are green turn to brown. And they wither in the wind, and they crumble in your hand ..."*

Biblical passages also present the precise honesty of life's progressive reality:

> *"As for man his days are as grass, as a flower of the field he flourishes. But the wind passes over it and it is gone. And its place shall know it no more." (Psalm 103:15)*

NEW WINTER VISTAS

But is all bleak? No. Winter, on the one hand, presents an apparent final end to the abundance and vitality of the prior seasons, *but also opens unexpected vistas.*

Although winter's arrival brings an end to aspects of life we've known in previous seasons, on the other hand it provides unexpected gifts that can't have been expected or even anticipated earlier. Although winter cold sets in, if, figuratively, we are 'clothed' in preparation for this new season's environment, we can now venture about and 'see' what couldn't be seen beforehand. *Trees and undergrowth, now stripped bare, reveal vistas concealed by the earlier clutter of (life's) vegetation.*

As way of example, I can remember during the summer one year, walking a hilly woodland area I hadn't ventured before, one of new overgrowth, *thick with profuse vegetation* (much as life itself can be). Density—like career mid-life—was everywhere! Thickness of summer humidity could be cut with a knife; drooping leaves and rambling vines seemed to put no limit on what could be crammed into that summer moment. Birds and critters further cluttered the scene—all in good ways, but clutter nonetheless. As I trekked on, what was to be seen ahead was little more than the next branchy vine, obscured woodchuck hole, or bramble bush masqueraded in leaf! The going was slow, but interesting—so much happening, so much to sense and occupy the mind.

Several months later, I remember experiencing a cold, wintry day. A "see forever" vivid blue sky and scattered cumulus clouds right-out made me smile (I still do thinking of the scene.) A brisk northwesterly breeze called me to hike to the same place I'd enjoyed earlier in summer. So with boots and walking stick in hand, I set out and ascended the same woodland knoll I remembered thick with all the vegetation.

Upon arriving, to my amazement, there before me lay a broad vista *and* distant hill lines beyond, all of which I'd had no idea existed when the incessant busyness of summer leaf and vine earlier obscured all this from view the recent summer. The air, as well, was so refreshingly different. The northwesterly breezes made summer and early fall's humidity only a memory. I walked on taking in the new views; breathing in the fresh, new air, and basking in the marvel of how one season so graciously gives way, silently, to the next. Somehow all was right with the world in those moments, even though death of summer's fullness and fall's glory must have taken place to present the winter upon me. I carefully studied the geography of land which earlier was veiled by summer growth and found lift to my soul that remains till this day.

There *are* new vistas in later life; even very later life. Our key is to now, maybe decades ahead of time, be encouraged we can take refuge against some of the negatives old age poses. In other words, there can be new vision and peace that accompanies the progressive withering of the outward frame. We do well to store this realty for possible due time in a season hence.

Can you see the *necessity* of progression here? What appears in winter *can only* be experienced if we've walked through the spring, summer, and fall seasons of life. Had I not walked the terrain in summer, come winter, no point of reference would have been established. The amazement and newness of the landscape's vista sensed in winter *was dependent on* life lived earlier. Although there was the loss of perishing vegetation there was an emergence of, literally, a new, comparatively quiet, but very real *horizon*.

Although woodland walks can be accomplished in any season, in real life we can only get to winter *if* we first experience the preceding three seasons. And the contrasts make all the difference.

Summer's Busyness; Winter's Simplicity

The 'vegetation' of life. Indeed, on those two woodland jaunts, the lack of leaves offered new perspective of a previously hidden view, but that same lack of clutter in winter also provided far less hassle and walking effort experienced in summer. The summer walk was downright difficult. Not only did thick undergrowth obstruct any sense of path to make the advance easier, but thick, humid air could nearly gag; ticks and chiggers added to the foray. Then there were the wild berry bushes whose prickly stickers could, as it were, nearly penetrate steel, let alone human flesh!

The clutter of summer's season of life becomes only a memory as winter clears the view.

On my winter walk, all the clutter was gone. In summer I'd made the same advance, blazing my own path, but winter not only removed obstacles, it offered new and memorable vistas and feelings. I can now look to life's winter with a balanced sense of expectancy: surely some loss of spring's vitality and summer's fullness , but also the gain of being able to see at a distance!

It takes all four seasons to fulfill the life of a single year.

In a real and accurate sense, as we are able to view our fall and winter seasons with the balance of loss and gain they possess, we can maturely, sensibly, proceed into the scene of later life with relative confidence. That confidence can best be built upon sound information, sensible comprehension, and subsequent planning which yield the best chances for success.

The retirement stage, inextricably linked to aging, and including the realism of life's termination, need not shatter a mature, balanced assessment of getting old. With a good approach to aging, a stillness and even confidence many never apprehend, can be attained. This inner settledness, however, can only occur when, instead of seeing later retirement life as a retirement ad poster-person or a perpetual vacation, we realistically acknowledge that aging and retirement are two sisters who, hand in hand, approach the last of life's developmental and final stages in relative peace and harmony.

Glossary of Terms and Principles

ambiguity/ambiguous—a word or concept open to more than one interpretation

boomer generation—the generation of 'baby boomers', born between 1946 and 1964

change & transition—<u>Change</u>: an outward circumstance that makes a situation in life very different; e.g., getting married, losing a parent, retiring. <u>Transition</u>: an inward effect; what we feel and how we react as result of the change in circumstances.

common ground—being of one mind with others; a foundation of mutual understanding

Creation—the physical world in which we live

developmental phase/developmental life stage—a broad segment of life years; e.g., adolescence, mid-life, retirement. "Developmental" implies in each segment we learn and grow. No segment is to be stagnant or counter-productive.

emotions—a state of being having to do with arousal of feelings; distinguished from other mental states such as cognitive thought and physical sensation (see "feelings")

feelings—an awareness; the power or ability of experiencing emotions

generational commonality/community—boomers unofficially forming a oneness; a camaraderie; a sense of being one because of similarities defined by a given generation of people

gerontology—the scientific study of the process of aging and the problems associated with it

identity—one's true characteristics as opposed to appearances

later-life—generally the retirement phase of life; post-career stage of living

materialism—the common doctrine or thinking that comfort, pleasure and wealth are the higher goals of life; to be more concerned with the material than with spiritual or intellectual goals or values

maximizing later-life—living a retirement centered on fulfillment as opposed to 'keeping busy'

New Retirement—a current buzz term differentiating previous generations retirement lifestyle from that of the current Boomer Generation; emphasis on life enrichment, self-reliance; purposefulness. (see "Old Retirement")

Old Retirement—a current buzz term typifying general retirement lifestyle characterized by all generations prior to the current Boomer Generation; emphasis generally on "keeping busy", general leisure, reliance on others. (see "New Retirement" and "self-forfeiture")

paradox—a seemingly contradictory statement or concept that may nonetheless be true; example—"Nobody goes to that restaurant; it's too crowded."; "The sounds of silence are deafening."

PC—political correctness

physical frame/outward frame—our physical body

reality—what we experience as being factual and real; being real, actual, or true

Retirement's Missing Link (the book title)—information and understanding about retirement that is unavailable from common sources; the "…rest of the story"

RSP (Retirement Success Profile)—an extensive, self-evaluating retirement-specific personal profile measuring individual retirement readiness; used concurrently with professional analysis and guidance. Find RSP at www.personal-retirement-planning.com

self-forfeiture—a giving up of self's purposefulness and direction. A common trait among retirees who live retirement within the Old Retirement paradigm (see "Old Retirement")

settledness—a favorite term of the author denoting peace at heart a pre-retiree can experience if solid preparation for later retirement is accomplished

truth—that which aligns with fact or reality; actual existence (see "Truth")

Truth—concrete spiritual concepts considered to be unequivocal; e.g., The Holy Scriptures, believed to be the true Word of God (see "truth")

Want more copies?

FRIENDS / FAMILY?

Who would appreciate honest retirement preparation ideas?

GIFTS–

- birthday
- holiday
- special "thinking of you"

for current retirees who could use a reading boost in their everyday retirement experience

Simply go to www.personal-retirement-planning.com and order per the instructions found there. Or contact us directly at:

Golden Years Publishing
2062 County Line Road
East Greenville, PA 18041

267-644-7506

Personal Checks accepted: $18.95 + $4.00 s/h

Thank you for your order!